READING *GODOT*

LOIS GORDON

Reading *Godot*

YALE UNIVERSITY PRESS NEW HAVEN AND LONDON

Designed by Rebecca Gibb. Set in Scala type by Keystone Typesetting, Inc. Printed in the United States of America by Vail-Ballou Press.

Library of Congress Cataloging-in-Publication Data
Gordon, Lois G.
Reading *Godot* / Lois G. Gordon.
p. cm.
Includes bibliographical references and index.
ISBN 0-300-09286-5 (alk. paper)
1. Beckett, Samuel, 1906–1989. En attendant Godot. I. Title.
PQ2603.E378 E644 2002
842'.914—dc21
2001006565

A catalogue record for this book is available from the British Library.

The paper in this book meets the guidelines for permanence and durability of the Committee on Production Guidelines for Book Longevity of the Council on Library Resources.

10 9 8 7 6 5 4 3 2 1

TO ALAN AND ROBERT

CONTENTS

ACKNOWLEDGMENTS

Acknowledging those who have helped me with my work on Samuel Beckett takes me back to graduate school when the Swift scholar Ricardo Quintana encouraged me to study Beckett. It is impressive, I think, that virtually everyone who had published on Beckett in those days still remains in the pantheon of Beckett's most distinguished critics: Ruby Cohn, Martin Esslin, Raymond Federman, John Fletcher, and Hugh Kenner. After Beckett won the Nobel Prize, the scholarship flourished. The abundance of talented people studying the man and his work, then and now, remains imposing. I hope my notes and bibliography will serve as an acknowledgment of my respect for and gratitude to the many thoughtful scholars who have continued the lively Beckett dialogue over the years.

I owe special mention to a few whose work or advice has been particularly useful in this book. Martha Fehsenfeld and Dougald McMillan provided an excellent commentary on Beckett's *Regiebuch* in *Beckett in the Theatre*. Their work on *Waiting for Godot* was based, in part, on the production notebooks in the Beckett Archive at the University of Reading, founded by James Knowlson. Knowlson's publication of the *Waiting for Godot* notebooks, the first volume in his *The Theatrical Notebooks of Samuel Beckett* series, was also immensely useful. Lois Oppenheim's *Directing Beckett,* a series of interviews with and essays by Beckett's directors, was a vital and provocative resource. Finally, Tom Bishop gave me generous access at New York University to the videos of the Schiller-Theater and San Quentin Theater Workshop productions of *Waiting for Godot*. Rick Cluchey's recollection of his work with Beckett was inspirational. The illustrations on pages 132–34 are courtesy of Martha Fehsenfeld.

It is my good fortune to have friends and colleagues who offered invaluable support and conversation, many of whose remarks about Beckett have remained with me over the years: Alec Reid, William York Tindall, Mel Friedman, Warren G. French, Laurence Wiley, Gottfried Büttner, Bernard Dick, Pauline Flanagan, Xerxes Mehta, Thomas Cousineau, Robert Levine, Ilene Engelmayer, Charlotte London, Marvin Rechter, and Barbara Deblat. I remain deeply grateful to my librarian-friends Eileen McIlvain, Judy Katz, and Laila Rogers.

Once again I acknowledge the talented people at Yale University Press, whose professionalism at every stage of production has been exemplary. Two people require special mention: Lawrence Kenney, for his highly insightful and meticulous manuscript editing, and Jonathan Brent, who even as executive editor of the press, remains the author's ideal friend.

Last but certainly not least I want to thank my husband, Alan, and my son, Robert, whose encouragement and suggestions were invaluable.

INTRODUCTION

The Form of Madness: A Sensible Mess

> One cannot speak anymore of being, one must speak only of the mess. When Heidegger and Sartre speak of a contrast between being and existence, they may be right. I don't know, but their language is too philosophical for me. I am not a philosopher. One can only speak of what is in front of him, and that now is simply the mess. . . . [It] invades our experience at every moment. It is there and it must be allowed [into art]. . . . What I am saying does not mean that there will henceforth be no form in art. It only means that there will be a new form and that this form will be of such a type that it admits the chaos and does not try to say that the chaos is really something else. The form and the chaos remain separate. . . . That is why the form itself becomes a preoccupation, because it exists as a problem separate from the material it accommodates. To find a form that accommodates the mess, that is the task of the artist now.
>
> *Samuel Beckett*

In the premodern era, religion explained both human nature and the human condition. By the end of World War II, philosophy and psychology had not so much destroyed the gospel as rewritten it in secular language. Freudianism and existentialism were exciting new paradigms of Western thought, and although their influence has declined, they provided the intellectual framework for many of the twentieth century's greatest artists, including Samuel Beckett.

Ironically, the outcome of the Freudian revolution in understanding human psychology was a view of the species a medieval monk would have found congenial. In the gospel according to Freud, humans beings are creatures instinctually given to "lust, murder, and cannibalism." Cultural institutions, including religion, Freud believed, are the species' forlorn efforts at restraining these biologically inborn impulses. For the monk, God was, of course, both the architect and redeemer of the shortcomings of human nature.

Even the prescriptions of classical psychoanalysis bear a striking similarity to the medieval sacraments, for here again the guilty dare not face their accuser. They lie down and stare at ceilings (instead of sitting in dark boxes) in the confession of their sin, and they direct their hope for salvation toward analysts (instead of God and his representatives). In both these seemingly distinctive rituals of expiation, humanity is presumed to be evil.

The existentialists proposed a different vision but one that also has its counterpart in the medieval experience. Here, the concept of the human situation, rather than human nature, would have been congenial to the medieval mind. Existentialists depict the anguish and loneliness of facing the void; they describe the emotional despair of dealing with the absence of a felt or verifiable moral order. So, too, in the *Varieties of Religious Experience,* William James describes how, at the height of the medieval synthesis, the fourteenth-century mystic struggled with a despairing sense of separation from God.

Estragon's declaration "We were all born mad" in *Waiting for Godot* may well be understood in both psychological and existential terms. This may be a modern version of original sin, for madness, many believe, is inherent in human nature. It is not a qualitatively different state from sanity, but rather the condition in which the ubiquitous forces of unreason break the fragile veneer of reason and burst into consciousness and bizarre, dereistic behavior. In sanity, these forces warp the facade, but reason manages to hold, except in dreams, slips of the tongue, and socially acceptable, overtly coherent, and often transparently rationalized forms of instinctual expression, like war and neurosis.

According to classical psychoanalysis, the infant is pure instinct, a creature of rage, lust, and narcissism, and the adult retains the infant as an eternal hidden engine operative beneath the cover of repression. The clinically mad by definition can no longer subdue that part of self. Repression, in other words, can no longer contain the repressed. Madness, as a universal human dimension, is thus a matter of form rather than content, a question of the balance of inner forces rather than their substance. It is the deepest inner experience of Everyone.

Differences between Freudianism and existentialism are numerous and obvious. In the main, however, like typical religious adherents, Freudians believe in an innate disposition, in "human nature," while existentialists are primarily concerned with the human situation or "human condition." They believe, in Sartre's familiar words, in existence rather than essence. Yet, while they do not hold that we are born with any predisposed moral or psychological nature, they assert that we are born *to* a condition, that is, into a world, that necessitates inevitable loneliness and anxiety. The absence of a verifiable order or Orderer—with language, intellect, and reason incapable of validating reality—impels a psychic dislocation as much as an intellectual bewilderment. In Beckett's terms, one feels one can't go on, yet one must go on. One requires purpose in a purposeless universe, identity in an estranged mind/body coupling. Of this, as well as of the intricate conflicts within the self, Beckett writes in *Waiting for Godot,* " 'Let's go.' (*They do not move.*)."

Ultimately, for both Freudians and existentialists, the natural state would seem to be one of alienation and disaffection, where madness is either one's inborn nature or the entirely irrational nature of the universe. In the end, "folly", to use one of Beckett's last words, would seem to be the most reasonable, normal, and appropriate description of the natural but futile striving to understand the world *or* self. In "what is the word," Beckett's last poem, its title echoing "In the beginning was the Word," Beckett begins,

> folly—
> folly for to—
> for to—
> what is the word—
> folly from this—
> all this—
> folly from all this—
> given—
> folly given all this—
>
> seeing—
> folly seeing all this—
> this—
> what is the word—
> this this—
> this this here—
> all this this here—
> folly given all this—

The following lines are "folly for to need to seem to glimpse / what where—" and Beckett continues, "afaint afar away over there what. . . ." The commitment to life, to "this this here," and the need to "glimpse" the "seen" and "afar away" can only be intimated as "folly"—a gentler word than "madness" but a refinement, all the same, of his earlier description in the above epigraph of "the mess."

"Folly" would also admit of the humor or self-mockery Beckett generously affords his most humble figures (and their witnesses, the audience, his readers) in their daily, heroic efforts at survival.

It was perhaps the widespread awareness of this mess or folly that contributed to the breakdown of traditional form in the several arts during the twentieth century. In music, initial assaults on form, dissonance, and diatonic music progressed to electronic cacophony and the randomness of the aleatory. In art, Cubist planes, Dada, and Surrealism led not just to the collage of commercial remnants heaped into pop art but also to the various forms of abstract and geometric expressionism, as well as the constructs designed through electronic media juxtaposed with fragments of traditional art forms. Arbitrariness, unreason, and madness—that is, human nature and the human condition—demanded expression, from Jackson Pollock's drip paintings (which display the unconscious in "action") to Jasper Johns' flags and maps (which question the meaning and function of the most ordinary icons of the everyday environment) and Ann Hamilton's cerebral/sensory installations that amass various materials encoded with personal meaning. The key to art's meaning or to the meaning of anything, for that matter, as Harold Pinter understated it in the 1960s, is that "verification remains impossible." At best, art sets two nonreferential mirrors into perpetual interaction.

In literature, the presence of the mess has been clear, from the use of stream of consciousness to explore the depths and intricacies of subjectivity, exemplified so boldly in James Joyce, to the work of more traditional prose stylists such as Saul Bellow, who portray life as an essentially deranged and deranging experience, suggesting that madness is an apt description of the human condition. The antihero, the individual no longer able to triumph in a moral sphere, has become the inevitable offspring of both Freudianism and existentialism: if one's instinctual nature mocks all efforts at nobility and if cosmic absurdity mocks all pretenses to moral certainty, then heroism can be only the rationalized product of self-deception or self-aggrandizement.

In the 1950s and 1960s, several highly regarded novels written in the picaresque formula, like *The Adventures of Augie March, Catch-22,* and *V,* resolved (or ignored) these philosophical and psychological issues by isolating the lusty, self-contained hero who, aware of both instinct and absurdity, set out to gratify the former while denying the latter. John Barth, Jorge Luis Borges, and Gabriel García Márquez confronted these weighty matters and juggled the simultaneous need for and futility of personal choice against both the purposive and fantastic inner and outer worlds. By the late 1960s and 1970s, the already extended boundaries of the traditional arts were pushed to new limits, as the postmoderns self-consciously obscured the line between author and audience and between objectivity and subjectivity. Writers like Robert Coover and Donald Barthelme sought to define the unconscious patterns the mind imposes on its various ordering systems, the way myths and language take shape from the struggle between logic, instinct, and the urge to communicate the incommunicable. Readers of these difficult new forms, like audiences of total theater, environmental and kinetic art—and any variety of "happening"—were asked to join in the creation of a kind of performance art, to partake of what John Cage had called the Yes-and-No total aesthetic experience. Alongside these new forms, literary criticism from hermeneutics to deconstruction made its bid to replace art as the mirror of nature. Writers of the 1980s and 1990s like Don DeLillo and David Foster Wallace continued the trend of the metafictionists and postmoderns. Others, such as Toni Morrison and Richard Ford, incorporated new poetic trends in their evocation of character and plot as they retained concrete situations of social and moral peril.

Throughout, the theater remained a remarkably fertile arena in which to explore and reflect the concerns with (1) the multiple components of self, (2) language as a means of constructing reality, and (3) the issue of moral survival in a contingent universe. In the 1940s and early 1950s, Arthur Miller and Tennessee Williams pursued traditional drama, and Sartre and Camus focused on existential matters. Other midcentury playwrights, however, such as Eugène Ionesco, Harold Pinter, Edward Albee, and, among the earliest, Samuel Beckett—practitioners of the then-labeled Theatre of the Absurd—further explored Camus' and Sartre's themes, but they incorporated into their art the emotional ramifications of the existential plight. Furthermore, they rendered these in the very language of the emotional life: of unconscious as well as conscious thought functioning. If rational, conscious discourse could be recorded, so could unconscious thought, as intuited by the artist and as recorded through psychoanalytic research and dream analysis. Beckett was at the forefront of this new dramatic rhetoric, having read Freud, worked with the Verticalists and Surrealists in Paris during the 1920s, undergone psychoanalysis in London in the 1930s, and, perhaps most important, having ardently befriended James Joyce, at work on *Finnegans Wake*. Beckett was also closely associated with a number of painters outside the Surrealist circle, including Bram van Velde and Jack B. Yeats, who, in their own work, were exploring the various levels of mind functioning.

Experimental efforts to portray the psyche were, of course, not unique. Strindberg, for example, had progressed from naturalism to dream techniques, as he displayed the power and chaos of the emotional life. But he never tried to articulate the specific vocabulary of unconscious experience. Pirandello had visualized the *illusions* of reality that camouflage deeper truths of murder, lust, and greed, but he too stopped short of holding the mirror up to unconscious thought patternings. And although their dramas failed, Surrealists like Roger Vitrac, Raymond Roussel, Robert Desnos, and Jean Cocteau attempted an art that bypassed logic in order to concretely render the unconscious, but they ignored the *simultaneous* operation of conscious and unconscious thinking.

One of the seminal works of the avant-garde was *Ubu Roi,* Alfred Jarry's portrait of a protagonist both devoid of moral qualms and a madman. Ubu was the personification of infantile rage and lust, human nature in its rawest form, as well as a man who, aware of the ultimate meaninglessness of life, chose evil over righteousness as the cornerstone of his being. Jarry's devoted advocate Antonin Artaud went so far as to envision a theater based on the ritual expression of aggression, on the very "automatism" of the liberated unconscious. For Artaud, traditional drama was a cover-up for authentic, underlying emotion, and unless form was altered entirely and emotion given total outlet, human experience could not be fully dramatized. Even before Artaud and Jarry, Mallarmé and the other French Symbolists who had fascinated Beckett during his Trinity College years conceived of a theater that would suspend intellectual appeal by staging metaphors of the dream state.

This kind of experimentation found its fruition in Beckett's uniquely poetic and seemingly elusive forms. Beckett went beyond surreal and expressionistic images and beyond rational dialogue, beyond any art form to date, in order to portray contingency and the absurd, operative both within and without: within the individual psyche and without, in the individual's external, cosmic environment. From his earliest works in the journal *transition,* such as "Sedendo and Quiescendo," Beckett incorporated the language of the inner, irrational life, alongside the language of philosophical investigation. In his greatest work, he became the spokesperson of the postwar age, and his *Waiting for Godot* took its place beside *The Waste Land* and *Ulysses* as the quintessential expression of the twentieth-century zeitgeist.

Beckett had himself been witness to the extremes of human nobility and degradation. Although raised in an affluent community and educated in elite schools and later surrounded by the greatest artists of his time, Beckett bore witness to a world of "murder and cannibalism," in Freud's terms. From his childhood in Dublin during the Easter Uprising of 1916 and World War I, through his experiences in London during the depths of the Depression, until World War II, when he was a Resistance fighter, Beckett had firsthand evidence of the underside of humanity: of mental and physical illness, of selfishness and opportunism in the guise of benevolence, and, of course, of the indescribable barbarity humans inflict upon one another. If his study of literature, philosophy, and religion, and their speculations about human nature, were at best a confirmation of the terrible life experiences he faced from childhood until the end of the war, then his personal relationships—not the least of which were the close family ties he cherished until his death—gave him a contrasting view of human nature. Beckett's friendships with a number of exceptionally generous and idealistic people, all defenders of the disenfranchised and devotees of what one called the "trinity of the true, the good, and the beautiful," reinforced in him the moral imperative that acts of kindness and altruism may transcend life's travails. Such was the life that shaped the man who, after World War II, began his personal "siege" and wrote some of the greatest work of the twentieth century.

The American reception of *Godot,* in 1953, one of bewilderment and frustration, was not unlike its earlier receptions in Paris and London and was only an intimation of the confusion and frequent anger Beckett's subsequent work would evoke. Audiences accustomed to the naturalistic work of Arthur Miller and Tennessee Williams frequently agreed with reviews that read "the thing is simply an exercise in logorrhea"; the play is the work of a man "who prefers puzzles to people"; Beckett's characters just stand there "with Existentialism on their faces."[1] Yet despite *Godot*'s cancellation in Washington, Boston, and Philadelphia, Grove's paperback printing of five thousand copies sold out before its official publication date, and Beckett soon found his home in the newly refurbished environs of

Off Broadway. The undisputed realization of a major new dramatic style emerged within academe; the quest for clarification began, and Beckett's concern with the human condition elicited most attention. The plays were defined in virtually every category of thought—as Christian, Marxist, existential, gnostic, mythic, parodic, ironic, Jungian—and the range of Beckett's comic inventiveness, from the vaudevillian to the scatological, the fantastic to the grotesque, was similarly investigated.[2]

Some critics sought an entirely new terminology.[3] Many of the earliest studies examined Beckett's literary and philosophical antecedents or focused on his heroes: they were Cartesian questers deprived of the certainty of "I am" while continuously in search of it; they were preoccupied with the verification of self and reality despite the limitations of logic and language.[4] In keeping with the styles of postmodern analysis and using the language of structuralism, deconstruction, and reader-response criticism, scholars then reacted to Beckett's handling of language, to his semantic and syntactic de- and reconstructions and rearrangements, as examples of the (fictive) re-creation of the devalued "I." Beckett was placed in the line of Wittgenstein, Heidegger, Saussure, and Derrida: if the limitations of his language were the limitations of his world, the universe was necessarily beyond cognition. The politics of silence became another fertile area of critical inquiry. Beckett criticism scoured a vast terrain of interesting issues.[5]

As Beckett's landscapes and language became increasingly reduced, his texts and their many revisions were further analyzed as conduits to pure being or personal revelation. His last plays were taken beyond metafictional and self-reflexive theorizing, with the result that stagecraft—light, music, or, for example, a character reading to a character reading to yet another character—became the focus of epistemological and aesthetic issues. The plays were viewed as poems or musical inventions, with production, once again, the key to meaning.[6] For some, through the purity of his forms, Beckett had reached the ambivalence of the Sublime. He had achieved "the silence, or the abyss, . . . the metaphysical or spiritual reality of existence at last exposed, beyond further illusion." He had transcended gnosticism in an assertion of human freedom, turning Schopenhauer's fragmentation and Will into Apollonian wholeness. He had achieved a kind of mystical or religious state of mind in transforming fictional space, the imaginary and the silent, into a magical place of closure.[7]

In most of these commentaries, Beckett remained essentially the philosopher: his work was read as the persistent attempt to grapple with the unknowable. Whether focusing on reduced or restructured plot, character, and language, on the various forms of parody or classical influence, on an utterly pared down yet poetic language or geometrically designed stagecraft, or on the postmodern Sublime—analyses most frequently turned to philosophical matters, to issues regarding the human condition. Beckett was described as the author of a meticulously designed existential language of uncertainty that served as a vehicle for personal mythmaking or as an intimation or unveiling of chaos or silence. His poetry may have been unspeakably beautiful, but it stood as a testimony of human industry in the face of terror.

Beckett's audiences, from the inmates at San Quentin and the children of Appalachia to academia's more sophisticated theatergoers, responded to his innovative "tragicomedy" in new ways. Here was, to be sure, the tragedy of humanity at the mercy of random, gratuitously kind or brutal inner and outer forces. But here was, as well, the comedy of humanity's repetitive, often ridiculous, acts of accommodation to the mess and to the personal neediness of others. Beckett's images of human persistence, along with his characters' repeated self-mockery as playthings in a world of cosmic emptiness, were irresistible.

As the subject of critical analysis, Beckett poses a difficult problem. He has created, to be sure, a unique dramatic and fictional idiom, and his innovative staging and linguistic arrangements give striking new definition to traditional genres. At the same time, Beckett's academic background and what appears to be the metaphysical preoccupation of his characters have made philosophical interpretation inevitable. Throughout his life, however, Beckett warned that he was not a philosopher; as his narrators frequently assert, "I'm a big talking ball, talking about things that do not exist, or that exist perhaps, impossible to know, beside the point"; and "Where now? When now? Who now? Unquestioning. I, say I."

While the body of Beckett criticism has been of immeasurable assistance in explaining the work, it has not dealt adequately with the psychological depths of his characters, with their emotional world—with Beckett's vision of human nature. Beckett's insistence upon his failure "to know," like his insistence that he is not a philosopher, may forewarn the critic as to the limits of philosophical commentary and perhaps provide a meaningful clue to this other vital aspect of his work.

What remains to be examined is that core or foundation that sustains each work's organic unity and, I believe, generates both its universal appeal and subsequent mystery and depth. I refer to that level of design akin to what Aristotle called soul, and others from Aquinas to Joyce called integrity, wholeness, radiance, and quidditas. For Nicolas Boileau and later Samuel Johnson, it was simply "je ne se quoi." What remains to be explored in Beckett is that level of artistry that reflects and touches the universal emotional life and elicits from the least to the most sophisticated audience a deep identification and powerful catharsis. It is perhaps from this that all meaningful philosophical issues arise, from this that the sudden and intuitive revelation of the infinite occurs, which Longinus, Kant, Nietzsche, and Burke define as the Sublime.

As Beckett states in the epigraph above, the aesthetic problem for the contemporary artist is stylistic: a new form is needed to accommodate the chaos of experience: "The mess invades our experience. . . . It is there and it must be allowed. . . . To find a form that accommodates the mess, that is the task of the artist now." Beckett's triumph, as I hope to illustrate, is that his greatest works (and I shall use *Waiting for Godot* as my primary example) discover this new form. Beckett incorporates the mess in its internal and external manifestations by portraying not just the rational mind involved in self- and worldly definition (the human situation), but also by portraying that mysterious, often turbulent zone of being that frequently invades rationality in order to liberate, victimize, or paralyze the individual (human nature). He incorporates what I earlier called the ubiquitous dimension of madness—not just in plot or context, as Dostoevsky, Kafka, Strindberg, Camus, and Sartre used it—but in its very *form,* as an ordering and structural principle.

Beckett's sophisticated understanding of total mental functioning is striking in the light of the major studies on the syntax and structure of conscious and unconscious thought process. One might think Beckett trained in this field, given the incisiveness of his knowledge of unconscious process and his evocation of the intertwining logical and unconscious mind. Clearly, his work at a mental institution and longtime friendship with the psychiatrist Geoffrey Thompson, in addition to his two-year analysis with the prominent psychiatrist W. R. Bion as well as his association with the Surrealists and the Joyces,[8] gave him ample opportunity to observe, absorb, and discuss the harmonies and dissonances of these two interpenetrating thought patterns. Beckett was also gifted as a language student and musician. Just as he never forgot paintings he had seen years earlier and repeated shapes and forms in his stage designs, so too he recalled and artistically utilized the cadences and linguistic patterns of irrational, schizophrenic conversation as he had studied and heard them. What emerges from this unique dramatic rhetoric, this intermingling of conscious and unconscious grammar and syntax, is thus more than an image of Cartesian duality, or the battle between the "I" and "me," or the heroic struggle to purify or understand the self or world, in spite of the Berkeleyan, Kantian, and Wittgensteinian paraphernalia attached to Beckett's language and his characters' perceptions. What emerges as well, alongside his extremes of madcap activity and silence, is a carefully choreographed display of rational and emotional levels of functioning. Beckett's characters may typically waver between knowledge and ignorance, but they also waver between rational, socialized, altruistic behavior and the aggressive, more narcissistic needs of self. Caught between extremes in identities so tidily described by E. M. Forster as the beast and the monk, the Beckett hero reveals how these seemingly contradictory dimensions operate in concert or conflict, or in any variety of combinations. Beckett's focus is ultimately what Lionel Trilling called the authenticity, rather than the sincerity, of self.

Beckett has undoubtedly responded to the same zeitgeist as W. B. Yeats, Eliot, Joyce, Sartre, Stravinsky, and Picasso: the fragmentation of accepted values or, as Walter Lippmann put it, "the death of the ancestral order of custom and authority." But he has also rejected their formal designs, their salvaging and piling up of a vast imagery of moral, spiritual, technological, and social disintegration, in the service of a new moral order. He has repudiated the modernists' mission, virtually Dantesque in scope, to recreate a meaningful world by scaffolding its fragments on to the symmetries of historical and mythic patterns. For Joyce, Eliot, and the others, the fractured present *could* ultimately be reconstructed in the terms of past tradition and past value systems. Theirs was an art of positive faith, implicitly based on the boundless power of human will.

The positive element in Beckett is more modest. It arises in the absence of any redemptive system, and because it is inevitably eclipsed by inner or outer forces, when it appears it is poignantly ennobling. When Beckett's figures lift themselves momentarily from the perplexity and terror of their fate, they attain a grand and tragic status.

In the main, however, Beckett's work focuses on the feeling of fragmentation and disintegration that occurs when one lives in the absence of theological or cultural assurances and when one functions within the a priori constraints of language and the psyche. From his earliest writing, even the youthful poems and short stories, his always sophisticated young journeymen were filled with a terrible longing for purpose and wholeness in a world devoid of absolutes. They were also always driven by allusive emotional needs. Unlike Eliot's and Joyce's modest but goal-directed heroes, testing old assumptions and shoring up fragments for future reassemblage, the Beckett quester always concluded in the environs in which he began. His circular philosophical meditations were always in counterpoint to his unchanging (and corresponding) circular inner life.

To accomplish such an elaborate portrait of the mind, which he best achieved in the plays, Beckett first experimented with fiction. He redesigned the omniscient author and monologue functions by creating a unique novelistic persona. He replaced traditional character and action with the fragmented self: with couples like Watt / Knott and Molloy / Moran, who were comparable to his dramatic figures Vladimir / Estragon, Krapp / the tapes. Each functioned not just as an entity in itself but also as the fluid half of a potentially integrated whole. Despite each half's discrete relationship to time, space, language, and even body movement, the heart of either the fictional or dramatic conflict was always each one's putative center and whether or not it was able to hold.

For many readers, Beckett's novel was too difficult a form in which to relate to the complex interstices of consciousness and the unconscious. In addition, the fractured self was easily obscured by the abstruse monologue format of the trilogy; in the earlier *Murphy* and *Watt,* it was overwhelmed by a self-conscious, self-reflexive, and at times ironic or unreliable omniscient voice. All the same, the novels and short stories addressed issues of isolation and fragmentation and were quests for both meaning and wholeness.

Drama proved a better format for particularizing the inner landscape. Lighting, sound effects, the timing of pauses, and even gesturing and diagonal or vertical movements and the level of voice intonation, in addition to the most basic elements of character, plot, and dialogue, could function as manifestations of a particular level of mental functioning. The most subtle detail—and Beckett's plays are known for their meticulous stage instructions—contributed to Beckett's intention and design, and each one, as in the trilogy, refined his portrayal of what it feels like to be bereft of a directing and empowering ideal and what it feels like to lack a centered, cohesive psyche.

Beckett's ability to give form to the universal self may explain why his audiences cut across national boundaries, social class, age, and education. Given the wide population his plays reach and the extraordinarily diverse responses they elicit, one is obliged to realize that these seemingly sparse, minimalist works are actually rich tapestries of evocative new poetic forms. His lyrical abbreviations and condensations of the inner emotional life go beyond even Proust's and Joyce's expansive creations. Beckett mirrors the generic and hence most far-reaching rhetoric of universal mental functioning. Each word, gesture, and movement is a vastly compact emotional stimulus to the audience to participate in and complete the work. This may also explain why Beckett has elicited such an immense amount of critical inquiry.

If great artists depict the universals of human experience, they also reflect particular epochs in the history of their culture. Beckett, to be sure, wrote in an age when questions regarding the benefits and limitations of will and reason had become prominent. Although a student of Descartes, Arnold Geulincx, Berkeley, Leibniz, and Kant, perhaps more than any of his contemporaries, Beckett concentrated on the emotional fallout of the rational-scientific quest, on the psychological consequences incumbent upon the pursuit of rationalism in a world devoid of consensually validated truths. That his focus on the emotional life may account for why his work deeply moves audiences is, however, not to ignore the philosophical implications of his art to which the bulk of Beckett scholarship has been addressed. Beckett's heroes go to great lengths illustrating the creative uses to which logic can be turned, and there is little doubt that these one-time scholars, philosophers, and writers are among his most poignant, often silly figures. In fact, the ironic implications of their buffoonery, along with their demonstrations of the limitations of language and logic, place them in the mainstream of contemporary philosophical and psychological thinking and in a quite dissimilar context from the protagonists of Joyce, Kafka, and Eliot. Through the self-reflexive irony of his characters, Beckett echoes the concerns raised by the great philosophers of our time, from Husserl and Heidegger to Foucault and Derrida. In his unique explorations of human nature and the human condition, Beckett shares these thinkers' preoccupation with the nature of mind, conscious and unconscious, as the basic organizer, interpreter, and responder to reality.

Beckett's characters struggle to survive in a world devoid of moral certainty and validated cultural norms, and then they experience the troubling consequences that such an engagement elicits: the blurred distinctions between words and meaning, good and evil, madness and sanity—in other words, the mess, as Beckett described it.

This relativism resounds in all Beckett's work, as it does throughout the intellectual and everyday life of our contemporary world. That is, after the exaltation of materialism and science, many intellectual disciplines, including psychology, philosophy, philosophy of science, and even physics, have had to contend with the disturbing threat of relativistic doubt, the difficulty of distinguishing fact from explanation as well as fact from fact. Werner Heisenberg and quantum physics, no less than Freud and Sartre, have demonstrated that the limits of our universe are determined by the limits of our measuring instruments, whether they are atomic clocks, blood pressure cups, or nouns and verbs.

Beckett, as the artist of the psychic distress born of relativism, stands in relation to our time much as Sophocles, Cervantes, Shakespeare, and Chekhov did to theirs: a spokesperson and questing, prophetic, empathetic recreator of the urge for order in a time of doubt and historical transformation.

ONE

The First Forty Years, 1906–46: Origins of a Vision and Form

Samuel Beckett began his creative "siege in the room" shortly after the siege of World War II and produced during that period his greatest works, including *Waiting for Godot, Molloy, Malone Dies,* and *The Unnamable.* Decorated for his activities in the Resistance, Beckett had fought against the atrocities of the war, although before that time he had borne witness to nearly half a century of human depredation and suffering. The parameters of his maturation included two world wars, two economic depressions (in Belfast and London), and two civil wars (in Ireland and in wartime France). Beckett observed the gradual spread of totalitarianism across much of the world and unrelenting campaigns of slaughter rising out of religious and ethnic prejudice. He also observed the panoply of human responses to these events: indifference, pettiness, megalomania, bravery, and self-sacrifice. He survived with a profound sense that evil cannot go unattended and that the defense of the good, whether in dramatic or modest action, gives dignity and meaning to life. He approached his personal siege with firsthand knowledge of humanity's rapacious, benevolent, and sometimes ridiculous potential. That his work would extend to the limits of tragedy and comedy, in a form he called tragicomedy, is the result, in many ways, of the vision he gained from his life experiences through 1946.

As an Irish citizen and neutral alien, Beckett did not have to take a position during the war, but, as he told others, he could not stand by with his arms folded and observe the suffering around him.[1] This explanation is of particular interest because when speaking of his happy childhood—"You might say I had a happy ["a very good"] childhood"—he was compelled to add, "But I was more aware of the unhappiness around me."[2] Beckett was an extraordinary man—modest, brilliant, gifted in several arts, loyal to his friends and family, uncommonly honest in his dealings with others, generous in the extreme, and exquisitely sensitive to suffering around him.

As the young child of affluent Protestant parents living in Foxrock, a Dublin suburb, Beckett was not insulated from the world around him by the privileges of his class. On the contrary, he was very much aware of both the civil and world war occurring during his childhood. His uncle, fighting with the British during the Great War, had been severely injured. Issues of alliance, of joining the British in World War I or of defying conscription to join the Irish insurgents at home, were continually debated. After the Easter Uprising, children ran about Dublin, where Beckett was attending private school, carrying Irish flags and singing nasty ditties about the English. Signs throughout the city proclaimed, "We will serve neither King nor Kaiser." The great political leader James Connolly had demanded that the Irish fight solely for their own independence, for "those natural rights which the British government [had] been asking them to die to win for Belgium."[3]

Civil war endured in Ireland long after the Great War ended, with shooting, curfews, ambushes, and murders in the street, and Beckett retained vivid memories of the uprising throughout his life. His father had taken him, when he was ten, to see Dublin in flames; attending school in Dublin, he regularly saw British soldiers carrying guns throughout the city. Newspapers were filled with details of the failed rebellion: the bloody retaliations of the Black and Tans, the subsequent installation of martial law, and the names of the many Irish who were deported, imprisoned, or executed before a firing squad. Connolly and Padraic Pearce had spoken of the need for sacrifice with irresistible rhetoric, and they described the sacred nature of their mission: "Men still know how to die for the holiest of all causes": "the practical brotherhood of the human race."[4] The sacrificial dimension of their calling was clear: "We recognize that of us, as of mankind before Calvary, it may truly be said: 'Without shedding of Blood there is no Redemption.' "[5] The notion of suffering redeemed through camaraderie and altruistic action would resound throughout Beckett's work and life. In *Waiting for Godot,* each figure repeats, in his own way, "To every man his little cross," aware that salvation arises alone from hearing the "cries for help" addressed to "all mankind" when "all mankind is us."

If the wars constrained Beckett's childhood happiness, so too did upper-class Foxrock. Beggars roamed the countryside, as they did in Dublin, and although Dublin had two "lunatic asylums," in Foxrock the mentally ill were kept at home. One such patient, near Beckett's house, was attended to by a keeper, a word that bothered the children because they knew this as a term used in the zoo. In addition, many retired service personnel lived in the Foxrock area because a war pensioners' hospital had been built near Beckett's house. As a result, Beckett often saw patients in various stages of physical and mental debilitation; one of Beckett's childhood friends recalls the children "witnessing" the torn bodies of veterans daily.[6]

In 1923, after the armistice and establishment of the Irish Free State, Beckett entered Trinity College, which, like his previous school, Portora, had been considerably changed by the recent wars. Courses and lectures such as the well-established Donnellen series recapitulated major issues arising out of the war. How, for example, could an Irishman fight in a world war alongside a Briton, who was his enemy in the civil war at home?

A great number of books on war and morality, science and religion were published during Beckett's Trinity years. Many, like E. B. Poulton's *Science and the Great War* and J. B. Hunt's *War, Religion and Science,* undermined righteous prewar ideals and emphasized the waste and despair of the present. The only remaining truths were the emptiness of the old morality and the devastating demonstrations of human bestiality. Perhaps Paul Fussell was correct in his later observation that World War I was the "archetypal origin" of the modern, ironic vision of life,[7] of the bitter reality that wars were made by men.[8]

The Great War ended, but a profound sense of indignity and injustice—alongside ongoing fighting in the civil war—continued for the Irish. The mayhem of the times quashed any residual illusions of Beckett's youth, of a world based on rational systems of rational adults, if not on rational reflections of a divine and just order. In this context, Beckett's remark that he "was raised almost a Quaker" but "soon lost faith . . . after leaving Trinity" is distinctly significant.

After Beckett was graduated from Trinity in 1927, he spent what he called a grim term teaching in Belfast—grim not only because of its severe economic depression but because of its terrible bigotry. The Civil Authorities (Special Powers) Act had given the Protestant authorities wide and often unjustifiable powers of arrest, search, detention, and internment. There was no doubt that to be Protestant was to be privileged and to be Catholic was to be visibly disenfranchised. Catholics were deprived of their jobs; marches of the unemployed were banned; restrictions increased on freedom of speech. It is understandable that Beckett, a Protestant Irishman who had witnessed a civil war at home, should find this a grim time. Again, brother was fighting brother, anticipating the internecine rivalries he would encounter in France during the Occupation. Here again were issues of religious discrimination that were to become, just a few years hence, the paramount obsession of Hitler's demented crusade. After Belfast, Beckett spent a year in Paris, which became his home in 1938. In the intervening years he lived mostly in London and traveled through prewar Germany. His first trip to Paris involved teaching at the École Normale Supérieure in fulfillment of one of his commencement honors at Trinity.

Paris in the 1920s was a dazzling city of frenetic energy and prodigious creativity. Yet for all its gaiety and sophistication, an underlying cynicism and sadness enveloped the city. Numerous commentators attribute its mercurial moods to the spiritual and emotional devastation of the Great War.[9] The grandest of human talents had been subverted to the meanest of human purposes; civilization had turned against and devoured itself.

The war had left the French, like people everywhere, in search of solutions to fill the void left by shattered prewar ideals. Older but still lively radical political communities like communism, socialism, and anarchism appealed to many. Also compelling were the philosophical ideas systematized by Nietzsche, Freud, and the phenomenologists. A number of relatively new aesthetic ideologies, vertiginous mixtures of Left and Right, were attractive as well: Futurism, Dadaism, the soon-to-be-fashionable Surrealism, and even the less political residual Cubism and early forms of Abstract Expressionism. Voices from abroad, of Vorticists and Suprematists, of Die Brücke and Der Blaue Reiter, gained a following. A revolution in the arts, with entirely new uses of color, harmony, and linearity, might counter the decadence, waste, and distortions of reality—the lies, as Hemingway called them—of earlier works and times.

Throughout Paris, the extremes of the avant-garde imagination were visible, along with the popular forms of Cézanne, van Gogh, and Gauguin. The 1928–29 season included at least four Cézanne shows, and Cézanne was an artist whose pictorial innovations would influence Beckett's stage designs. On exhibition were the Cubists and their Fauve successors, Picasso's new guitars, constructed now of painted metal, rather than paper, the biomorphic and geometric abstractions of Arp and Miró, and Mondrian's slick, intellectual puzzles. Visible as well, even in their many reproductions, were Duchamp's "readymades" and his goateed Mona Lisa as well as Brancusi's highly polished, elegant *Bird in Space,* at one and the same time abstract and representational. Roger Vitrac and Antonin Artaud, famed for holding the mirror up to the unconscious, founded Theatre Alfred Jarry in 1927. Sergey Eisenstein's experimental cinematography and the avant-garde compositions of Alban Berg, Arnold Schoenberg, and George Antheil were gaining broad attention. A new arrival from grim Belfast could only feel relief in the dynamic environs of Paris.

The visual and aural imagery of the new arts had a powerful effect on Beckett's work. His photographic memory enabled him, years later, to duplicate in his stage settings and in his productions the design of paintings he had not seen for decades. Techniques of nonlinearity in painting, accomplished through image fragmentation, dream imagery, and the intentional use of blank canvas—like atonal music achieved through the statistical arrangement of notes and incorporation of silence—influenced his use of language, gesture, and stage setting. The findings of the New Science concerning relativity, like those of the new linguists regarding the ambiguity of language, complemented the artistic revolution occurring around him.

The major artistic statements of Paris in 1928 emanated from the Surrealists, and they had a profound impact on Beckett. The Surrealists had found a broad and encompassing salvation in psychoanalysis. To them, Freud explained civilization and its discontents at the same time that he offered a kind of metaphysics for the exile, adrift amidst the recent loss of religious, social, and family values. Psychoanalysis promised an inner coherence to fill the personal or cosmic loneliness of the times. It also validated the "automatic" formulas of the new spontaneous and "pure" art forms.

Primarily devoted to unifying the inner and outer worlds, the artistic goals of the Surrealists, as their spokesperson, André Breton, expressed them, were "pure psychic automatism, . . . the real process of thought, [without] reason and . . . esthetic or moral preoccupation."[10] Many Surrealists published in Eugène Jolas's prestigious *transition,* which, when Beckett arrived, was chiefly associated with Gertrude Stein and James Joyce. Joyce published seventeen installments of *Work in Progress* (later, *Finnegans Wake*) there. Beckett soon came to work at and publish in *transition.*

Many of Jolas's goals in publishing *transition* were identical to those of the Surrealists. He demanded a "Revolution of the Word" and insisted that the artist create a language to unite personal, inner experience with the social world and cosmos. Pure poetry, he and the Surrealists declared, is "a lyrical absolute that seeks an a priori reality within ourselves alone." In an issue with one of Beckett's earliest pieces, "For Future Reference," *transition* included essays by Jung and Jolas on the importance of the dream life.[11]

In the "Poetry is Vertical" issue, which included Beckett's short story "Sedendo and Quiescendo," Jolas published the Verticalist Manifesto, signed by nine artists, including Beckett. An interesting blend of Jolas, Freud, and Jung, the manifesto called for the "hegemony of the inner life over the outer life."[12] For Jolas, a unifying mythos of dream and external would reveal the universal self in relation to instinctive, primal consciousness and the transcendent unity connecting all things.

That Jolas's and the Surrealists' primary goal was the "hegemony of the inner life over the outer life" is important in understanding Beckett's later use of unconscious thought functioning. In the trilogy, for example, Beckett set up a universal and "transcendental 'I,' " but instead of identifying a unifying mythos, he focused on the I's "final disintegration" in the very act of measuring itself. Each of his heroes was connected in the novels; in search of an irreducible self or voice, each became the refinement of his previous persona and moved to silence in the impossible quest of reaching the core of inner and outer reality. Only when Beckett began his dramatic writing did he achieve the balance between dream and reality; he also created a transcendent I—although, as we shall see, his conception of transcendence included the inner and outer self, not Jolas's or Breton's mystical, if temporary, synthesis.

As early as 1919, Breton had recognized that the mind has a continuous thought process that exists below consciousness, which Freud had called "primary process." Breton had studied Freud's writings and worked at the Charcot Clinic, where Freud had once been in attendance. Focusing on Freud's dream theory, he made the subtle observation that through the continuous operation of subterranean thought, the mind was naturally, as Lionel Trilling later phrased it, "a poetry-making organ." With its techniques of condensation, symbolism, and ambiguity and with its redefinition of time and space, poetry was "indigenous" to the very constitution of the unconscious mind.[13] Breton thus set forth as the first tenet of Surrealism the artist's obligation to retain the purity of unconscious thought process, which could be accomplished through automatic writing, without conscious control or awareness. He also proposed a series of other techniques by which the rational mind could be kept at bay. By the time Beckett began his association with *transition,* Breton's notions of how reality and dream recreate and reenergize one another had been much discussed.

In addition, bridging Beckett's past and present, his close association with the Surrealists allowed him to observe their exposure of the false dreams and hollow values that had produced the terrible war. Many figures, including André Masson, Max Ernst, Paul Éluard, Benjamin Péret, Breton, and Louis Aragon, had served in it, and many now defined their revolutionary art as a diatribe against the war; a number wrote commentaries on the war's spiritual and physical mutilations. In short, the Great War was an abiding topic of conversation in the Paris of 1928.[14]

Beckett's contact with the painters and writers who gathered around Breton introduced him not only to a variety of interesting new art forms, but to an entirely new body of ideas. Their idealism regarding the connectedness of all experience is apparent in "Assumption," in which Beckett's hero aspires to their *point sublime* of inner and outer revelation, although this is unique in the Beckett oeuvre.[15] Despite their Marxist interests, of little appeal to the young Beckett, the Surrealists wished to reconcile traditional contrarieties and dualities and to integrate chance, mystery, and mysticism in their quest to link opposites, like the inner and outer world, the conscious and unconscious life. Theirs was an art of constant flux and metamorphosis, as in dreams, where image and meaning continually connect and separate, where a sense of transcendence or wholeness mingles with a sense of the fragile and tentative. They pursued as well new parameters of time as it operates on both unconscious and conscious levels, for they strongly believed that the unconscious recreates external reality, just as the external world refuels the inner one.

In the bookstores of Montparnasse, artists of all nationalities discussed the radically new perceptions of reality and self in the areas of science, philosophy, psychology, linguistics, and art. Bertrand Russell and Alfred North Whitehead might have established, in a single system, all the valid principles of mathematical reasoning, a set of axioms upon which all rules would follow. But others, like Werner Heisenberg and Kurt Gödel, were pursuing their claim that the observer influences the observed and that any axiomatic system has undecidable propositions (for example, although we ought to be able to see ourselves in a mirror, we cannot see ourselves with closed eyes). These and other bookshops in Paris stocked the most talked-about authors, including Heidegger, Wittgenstein, Saussure, Ernst

Cassirer, Arthur Eddington, Jung, Freud, and Yeats. Not only did Beckett spend a great deal of time in these shops, but, as one commentator reports, "During this period [he] was obviously engaged in reading everything he could lay his hands on."[16]

In addition to meeting Jolas and the Surrealists and then working on and publishing in the little magazines, Beckett began or renewed several important friendships in Paris, often with people he idolized, absorbing and incorporating from them specific interests and commitments (and, on occasion, mannerisms) that would last a lifetime. Beckett met up again with Alfred Péron, whom he had known at Trinity, and they renewed their lengthy conversations on art, literature, and language. When Beckett moved to Paris in the late 1930s their relationship became so close that Péron involved him in the Resistance; Péron was subsequently captured and tortured by the Nazis.

The poet and future art critic Thomas McGreevy was a new acquaintance who became an intimate, lifelong friend. Wounded during World War I, the sophisticated, older (by ten years) McGreevy introduced Beckett to the circle of Dublin expatriates, as well as to many of Paris's most celebrated intellectuals, including Joyce. One learns as much about McGreevy in reading his commentaries on Jack B. Yeats, Richard Addington, Eliot, Leonardo, and Poussin as one learns about his subjects; he was a forthright idealist in advocating universal human rights and in believing that what matters "in art as in life [is] the classical trinity of the true, the good, and the beautiful."

Through McGreevy and Joyce, Beckett's literary circles soon widened. He met Valéry, Romains, Adrienne Monnier, Paul Léon, William Butler Yeats and his younger brother Jack, Eliot, George Reavy, Samuel Putnam, and many others. The profound effect of Joyce, twenty-four years Beckett's senior, cannot be overstated.

Joyce had three holy commitments: art, family, and friends. And as numerous memoirs testify, he was a very generous man with a profoundly humanitarian bent; he was also, to the surprise of many, extremely political. He was a devout Parnellite in his youth and, as an adult, was tortured by the knowledge of injustice occurring anywhere. He followed the politics of the cities in which he resided; his letters reveal his unwavering concern with the plight of the Jews during World War II. He was immensely proud to have created Leopold Bloom as his hero in *Ulysses;* he thought the *Odyssey* to be a Semitic poem.[17] Joyce had numerous Jewish friends who, in the passage of years, became Beckett's close friends as well.

Although Beckett adored his father, Joyce, despite his own prolonged personal and family suffering, came to function as a second father, encouraging his work and providing him with a model of the artist's commitment to his craft.[18] Perhaps in understanding this relationship, one might conjecture that Joyce found in Beckett a whole child, a young person he could truly help (he had fiercely tried to advance both his son's and daughter's careers), just as Beckett found in him a fatherly figure who was entirely approving. Joyce also found in Beckett a unique intelligence that understood and appreciated his work; many of Joyce's friends admitted they did not understand his new fiction.

Perhaps another reason for Beckett and Joyce's close association was that the older man recognized in Beckett an idealized image of himself as a youth. There were physical resemblances, and they had had any number of similar childhood interests and experiences.[19] But as parents sometimes relive in their children their unfulfilled youth, Joyce may have vicariously experienced in Beckett's filial devotion the feelings he had never overtly expressed to his beloved father.

By the end of the 1930s, after Beckett moved to Paris, his relationship with Joyce was so close that Joyce thought of him as his child.[20] Beckett began to imitate Joyce's personal mannerisms: his smoking, his posture when sitting, and even his choice of shoes. The two walked together and spent evenings in intellectual discussion and in sharing their family and moral values. Beckett learned about Joyce's onerous publishing experiences and about artistic forbearance. He observed the modesty of great celebrity: "Joyce met [people] face to face, as unassuming in his behavior as he was uncompromising in his aims. People lionized him but he would not roar." He once said to an academic who wanted to exalt him, "Don't make a hero out of me. I'm only a simple middle-class man."[21]

As Beckett himself was to be, Joyce was uncommonly supportive of both friends and aspiring young artists. Yeats and Pound had encouraged him to publish; he was encouraging Beckett and numerous others. Beckett, too, would become a mentor to many young writers, including Harold Pinter, who never produced or published a play until Beckett had read it. It was as though a legacy of respect and kindness were being passed from one generation to the next.

Regardless of his personal sorrows, Joyce always exercised a sense of humor, one that had no sniggering defeatism in it.[22] Even in moments of silence and pessimism, there was inevitably a "festive pause" when Joyce would start dancing and singing with whirling arms, high-kicking legs, grotesque capers, and coy grimaces. Such behavior corresponds to the transformations he was effecting in his art, intermingling matter and spirit, conquering tragedy through humor. Beckett, like Joyce, would come to understand humor as a defense against life's tribulations.

These traits persisted in the older Joyce, when he resisted his daughter Lucia's institutionalization and worried about a second world war. Even in his blackest moods, he retained concern for others and a wry sense of humor. Immersed as he was in writing, Joyce well understood the cycles of joy and sadness. His response, as an ordinary person and as an artist, was that of the healing comedian.

Within a short period, Beckett wrote several pieces. His ninety-eight-line poem "Whoroscope" won a prize when submitted to Nancy Cunard's Hours Press; Cunard had been closely associated with the Surrealists. Beckett also wrote *Proust,* one of the first in-depth studies of *A la recherche;* many of its remarks are reflected in Beckett's later work, particularly those insisting that form and content be one; that people adjust to the ordeals of survival by engaging in lives of habit; and that the only artistic avenue available to the artist, if intent on capturing the reality or the authenticity of being, is through the "excavation" of the unconscious life during moments of "latent consciousness," over which one lacks rational control. These intuitive, emotional explorations are "explosive" and "unruly"; they "cannot be importuned." They bring one in contact with the purest and least diluted part of self, and one remains powerless over the source from which they emanate.

Beckett's earlier essay in "Our Exagmination Round His Factification for Incamination . . . ," on Joyce's *Work in Progress,* foreshadowed *Proust* and his later work as well. Here, Beckett praises Joyce, as he would Proust, for his inseparability of form and content. Again he indicates the import of the inner mental landscape as the subject and form of art, as well as his awareness of the artist's awesome task in forging a language to serve this function. Joyce had explained to Beckett, "I wished to invade the world of dreams" and "I have put the language to sleep."[23] Beckett's essay functioned to clarify related goals of the *transition* Verticalists and Revolution of the Word proponents. Form and subject in Beckett's work would also be unified, as conscious and unconscious thought patterns (dreams) would reflect the excavation of the deepest core of self.

Joyce was uncanny in his understanding of these excavations, which were similar to Freud's revelations. To everyone's wonder, Joyce could follow his daughter's schizophrenic speech; she spoke in a form over which he had control. What mystified Joyce (and later Beckett) was not the world of the unconscious but the world of logic. "Why all this fuss and bother about the mystery of the unconscious?" Joyce asked. "What about the mystery of the conscious?"[24]

Beckett's relationship with Joyce and others, like his new career as a writer and his association with Paris's avant-garde, occurred during one of the world's most ignominious periods. The era marked the rise of totalitarianism throughout the world. The press detailed Hitler's escalating brutality against the Jews, reporting on concentration camps as early as 1933, and Germany's gradual takeover of European nations. The arrogant Hitler encouraged wide coverage of his various steps toward ethnic purification. Newspapers not only accommodated; many, in their editorial policies, reflected the indifference of most of the world.

Between Beckett's first and final move to Paris, he spent a brief period in Dublin. His college honors required that he follow two years of teaching at the École by three more at Trinity. Beckett did not like teaching and, in his own words, "behaved very badly: I ran away to the Continent and resigned." As he explained, he could not tolerate the "hateful comedy of lecturing . . . to others" what he did not know himself.[25]

Beckett's most important friendship during this period was with the painter Jack B. Yeats, thirty-five years his senior. Here was another older Irish artist with whom he could identify. The two shared a deep compassion for the alienated and disenfranchised, and they manifested this in remarkably similar artistic subjects and settings.

Since his youth, Yeats had been outspoken in the cause of Irish independence, but by the time of the Irish civil war and World War I he was overcome by the grotesqueries and bloodshed of world events. The war that broke out in Ireland after the British left in 1922, the defeat of Republican forces, and the south's transformation into a British dominion—with Ireland, in essence, still paying allegiance to the Crown—left Yeats totally disillusioned. By 1929–30, he had abandoned the politically and socially realistic images that marked his early style. He also began a career as a novelist. During this period he and Beckett became friends.

In his new paintings, Yeats reworked thirty-year-old political sketches to convey the inherent contradictions of the human condition. His images grew increasingly complex and resistant to sum-mary. Experimenting with opacity and the diffusion of linearity, he released himself from his earliest associations with the concrete image. Eventually, memory, that is, the concrete experience, and the dream and free associative state became inseparable, and he used the interplay of image and painterly texture to convey this complex condition of thought. As removed as he had been from the Surrealists, Verticalists, and other avant-garde movements on the Continent, he evolved an esthetic that in many ways echoed theirs. He sought to exteriorize the twilight area between fact and possibility, experience and illusion—experience as a product of conscious and unconscious response. Like Joyce in his manipulations of dream language in *Finnegans Wake,* Yeats used paint to evoke the way experience and objects appear before they are categorized in the rational mind. Later Beckett analogically wrote in *The Unnamable,* "You must say words, as long as there are any, until they find me, until they say me strange pain strange sin."

The ephemerality of human experience remained Yeats's consuming theme, with humanity now obliged to come to terms with itself in an environment free of external interference. His figures, often the socially oppressed or clowns, were subject to the indifference of nature or to forces beyond nature. Yeats then created images without specific backgrounding or clear-cut referents. Here was the human condition in its most authentic state, the self within the self. Conflict occurred in the private forums of being, where individuals do battle with the wild, uncompromising nature of an unknowable reality.

In Yeats's last images, he accomplished goals similar to those of the Verticalists. He reduced the artist's control of his universe to zero, aware of both the indeterminacy of meaning and self-knowledge at the same time as he accepted the interplay of conscious and unconscious thought. He realized that at best he could capture only "process" or the "stages of the image."[26] Hence, his lonely vagabonds, torn between promise and regret, inhabitants of life-contemporaneous-with-death, were frequently painted at twilight. This was Yeats's visual expression of the life of words "half-said . . . and even quarter said,"[27] his expression of the human tragedy—in Beckett's words, the elemental "sin of birth" into "impotence" and "ignorance," humankind on the isthmus between knowledge and powerlessness. To Beckett, Yeats had excavated those "perilous zones of being" in an effort to evoke that which eludes definition: "What is incomparable . . . is [his] sending us back to the darkest part of the spirit, [to] the great internal reality."[28]

After leaving Trinity, at the end of 1931, Beckett visited his family in Kassel, Germany. His cousin Peggy, about whom much has been speculated regarding their romantic attachment, had begun to show signs of the tuberculosis that would soon take her life. He returned to Paris in March 1932, but his stay was unexpectedly terminated in May, when the French president, Paul Doumer, was assassinated. Beckett's papers were not in order, and because he lacked a valid *carte de séjour,* or permanent resident status, he was forced to leave the country, and he returned to Dublin.

Beckett moved to London at the end of 1933, where he remained for nearly three years.[29] These were, as he put it, bad years—"bad in every way."[30] Perhaps most critical was the death of his father in June, shortly after the death of his beloved cousin Peggy. Despite his geographical distance from Joyce, Beckett was also deeply grieved to hear of Joyce's tribulations. Joyce was now compelled to commit Lucia to a sanitorium, and, nearly blind in his right eye and with minimal vision in his left, he had been advised to undergo yet another eye surgery. In addition, Joyce had become obsessed with the pornography trial of *Ulysses,* and his insomnia and the stomach ailment that ultimately took his life grew more severe.

Any of these personal events might have been sufficiently grave to depress Beckett, but he had professional problems as well. A teaching career was now unthinkable, and although he had begun to establish a literary reputation in Paris, the forced move out of France was deeply disruptive. Finally, and of no small consequence, Beckett moved to depression London during the "devil's decade." He witnessed not only vast starvation and poverty and many useless marches once again, but also the government's vast indifference to momentous cries for help. He experienced ethnic prejudice, as well: "They always know you're an Irishman. [Their] tone changes. The taximan says, 'another sixpence, Pat.' They call you Pat."[31]

Beckett's exile, in every instance, seems to have elicited his exquisite sensitivity to the suffering around him. If, during his happy childhood, he was affected by the plight of vagrants, the mentally ill, and the wounded veterans of World War I, and later, by the poverty and discrimination in Belfast, the sheer magnitude of destitution in depression London intensified his unhappiness. At about this time, Beckett's beloved half-Jewish uncle, Peggy's father, felt sufficiently threatened by Nazi activity to leave Germany. Beckett had long been interested in the Jewish plight. Joyce had frequently spoken of himself as a Jew, and he equated the Jews and Irish as persecuted peoples, as mentioned above. And in London during 1933, the press was filled with headlines regarding the beginning of Hitler's consecrated preparation to conquer the civilized world, including Nazi bloodbaths, Nuremberg rallies, book burnings, and separate schools for Jewish children. As Richard Ellmann noted, forty years after the war the subject of Jewish suffering made Beckett weep.[32] A line from *Waiting for Godot* reflects the sensibility of one keenly aware of the different fates life bestows: "Remark that I might just as well have been in his shoes and he in mine. If chance had not willed otherwise."

Beckett did survive the terrible London crisis. He underwent psychoanalysis, developed sustaining friendships, and read a great deal. He pursued a career in journalism, writing scholarly and literary reviews; he published translations[33] and began his novel *Murphy*. His first collection of short stories, *More Pricks than Kicks*—some of which were reworkings of the unfinished *Dream of Fair to Middling*

Women—and his cycle of thirteen poems, *Echo's Bones and Other Precipitates,* were published during this period.[34]

Beckett witnessed, during these London years, a transformation of the English cultural scene that proved salubrious to his personal and artistic growth. The years 1933–34 were pivotal in English stage history because of new production and acting styles initiated for the most part by John Gielgud and then Laurence Olivier. Old-style romance and sword-and-dagger panache, uninspired diction, and self-conscious, feigned emotion were replaced by simpler staging and a focus on the text, on slower and clearer diction, and on gesture and carriage. With the concentration on elocution and the use of voice came an emphasis on the spoken word. The distinctly new styles of acting alerted Beckett to new possibilities in the dramatic-lyric form.

The French Surrealists arrived in London in 1935 to assist in the long-awaited celebration of their English counterparts the following year. Beckett had been in frequent contact with the artists connected with the great exhibition, which Breton and Eluard attended. The English Surrealists also had found a way of dealing with reality in an art that exalted the dream as a creative source, "the kingdom of the irrational within ourselves";[35] they too held a credo that was curiously compatible with psychoanalysis, which Beckett was now experiencing firsthand in his analysis with W. H. Bion.

Beckett was a patient of Bion at the Tavistock Clinic; Bion's psychoanalytic practice at the time consisted of shepherding patients through various stages of dream experience to self-knowledge. An unusually erudite man, Bion had mastered the philosophy of H. J. Patou and written numerous works on Kant, justice, reason, perception, and time;[36] he had also written an autobiography that recounted his demoralization as a soldier.

Bion's main goal in analysis was to assist his patients in moving from what he called the alpha to the omega stage, the point of "One-ment" or "O"[37]—perhaps the origin of the "o" in "Godot." Rather than a cure, the process was a probing of self aimed at personal integration. As Bion explained, analysis was self-revelatory through dream analysis. "Cure or improvement," he wrote," is both "irrelevant and undesirable."[38] Onement involved a journey to the ineffable, absolute reality and unity of the fragmented self. Because it was a religious or mystical experience, one's knowledge of O could barely be translated into language.

As a part of Bion's therapy, and accompanying each of his books, was a grid (his term), an elaborate notational chart that indicated the various therapeutic stages one might take toward the O state. *A*, or alpha, for example, indicated when patients set aside memory in the gestation of dream formation; *B*, or beta, indicated their inability to use *A* properly, for in unsuccessfully dealing with memory and sense impressions, they might be led to feelings of persecution.[39] *K* indicated the words or analogies artists and great leaders might speak at having attained the O stage.

Bion supported many of Freud's clinical findings. He agreed, for example, that the language of the unconscious or of dream experience was the everyday speech of schizophrenics[40]—that schizophrenics live in a continual dream state. He also worked through Freud's tentativeness toward the life and death instinct in *Civilization and its Discontents*.[41] Like Jung, however, Bion was interested in the collective unconscious, and this was of particular interest to Beckett, for he had considered writing his Trinity thesis on Romains and the Unanimistes and their belief in a preexisting moral sensibility.

By 1933, Beckett had read both Freud and Jung. About that time he visited his psychiatrist friend Geoffrey Thompson in his London training hospital, Bethlehem Royal and took a job there for a year as an attendant, an experience "that influenced him very much."[42] By the end of his two-year analysis, Beckett was once again discussing the nature of mental functioning with Thompson, as the two visited the wards together and reflected on the language and behavior of the mentally ill. Given Bion's emphasis on symbolic language and dream analysis, as well as Beckett's own reading of Freud and Jung and his experiences with Joyce's daughter, Beckett was observing the dream speech of the institutionalized patients, which he would use in his later work, just as Bion's grid points would provide a profile of many of his characters.

In 1935, Beckett attended a lecture at the Tavistock and heard Jung describe the healthy unconscious as an unknown collection of fragmented selves to which the artist gives form in fictional characters. Jung also expounded on the anatomy of unconscious process and how it expands or asserts itself in normal thought function through increasingly lightened circles of energy. Its deepest part, the collective unconscious, occupies the darkest, smallest circle, he said. Schizophrenics, who function continuously in unconscious thought process, live, so to speak, in the realm of darkness. The similarities of Bion's concept, with its metaphors of light and dark,to the mystical images of Dante, Plato, Schopenhauer, and Leibniz are striking.

Beckett left London shortly before Christmas and returned to Dublin. He took on odd jobs like tutoring and spent a period of time reading at the Trinity College library. He was determined to complete *Murphy,* which was to become his first published novel (1938). It is a funny book about a jobless young Dublin man who moves to London, in fact, to the same area in which its author had just lived, and who strives for the total separation and control of mind from body. Murphy works in a mental institution and yearns to attain a state like the patients' "self-immersed indifference to the contingencies of the contingent world." They seem to have reached a Jungian or Bion-like state of Onement that unites all fragments: the "silence of the universe," in which "light and dark [do] not clash, nor alternate, nor fade nor lighten." Murphy, however, who suffers from heart, foot, and neck problems, remains tied to personal and amorous connections and is incapable of freeing himself from time and place. Bound to the flux, commotion, and light of ordinary experience, he resubjects himself to the accidents of the physical world, which conclude with his ashes being strewn on a barroom floor amidst sawdust and cigarette butts.

Beckett made a short trip to Dublin after leaving London and then traveled extensively through Germany.[43] Although he spent a great deal of time looking at art, the primary reason for the trip was his need to come to terms with Germany as a nation. He had long felt a deep sense of affection for the country, spending considerable time there with his family, during which he was introduced to some of the century's greatest art; the German language had also been part of his Trinity concentration. The trip functioned as a means of verifying the increasingly terrible reports he had read about the moral descent of the German citizenry. He had to see for himself the condition of the civilization he had both studied and respected.

According to Beckett's close friend Gottfried Büttner, the trip was partially a continuation of his education. Beckett had read Eduard von Hartmann, "who opened the debate on the notion of the subconscious." The trip in addition furthered his art education, as he traveled from one gallery to another.[44] Beckett was interested in the Germany of the Surrealists. As Anna Balakian explains, the Surrealists were Germanophiles during the 1920s and until Hitler came to power.[45] Until he condemned Hitler in 1935, Breton was thoroughly fascinated with the marvelous country that had given birth to and nurtured Kant, Hegel, Ludwig Feuerbach, and Marx. Hegel had, after all, expressed his belief in the inner unity of contradictory phenomena and defined knowledge as the linking of thought and object. The Surrealists had also sought unity among contradictions—of the self and world, the concrete and the abstract. Beckett wished to visit the home of this important art movement.

What Beckett came to observe was a society held in thrall by a false idol in whose name all manner of brutality was rationalized as sacred. He visited and learned of the despicable treatment given the great art critic Willi Grohmann. He witnessed the dangers of an ideological aesthetic. Hitler and Goebbels, both frustrated artists, were using art as a political instrument, as a reflection of and means toward racial superiority and domination. Perhaps Beckett's awareness of this played a role in his later fashioning a form that was largely free of concrete place, person, and partisan political ideology.

Finally, as Büttner suggests, Beckett visited Germany in an attempt to describe and come to terms with the "desolate age." Schopenhauer, "one of the few that really matter," said Beckett, might have provided him with a framework for understanding the terrible world around him. *The World as Will and Idea* might have accounted for the perverse use of power that now dominated German culture. Later, as Beckett wrote *Waiting for Godot,* Büttner continues, "the monsters lurking in each and every one of us" may "well have emerged from the depths of [his] memories."

Büttner says that Beckett's long correspondence with him revealed that the trip not only exposed the "cultural catastrophe of the rising Nazi leadership," but also helped Beckett clarify his worldview and presented another "pathway" to his "innermost self." Beckett's visits to cemeteries reinforced his sense of human transience and affirmed the wisdom of the ages—the advice of the Italian Giacomo Leopardi, for example, whom Beckett frequently quoted—regarding the stoicism necessary to meet the gloom of experience. In sum, the German journey, Büttner concludes, contributed to Beckett's "hard-won equanimity" and "admirable mastery of the [desolate] *conditio humana* of modern times." It was preparatory for the tests that would follow of his physical and creative ability to survive.

Once in Germany, Beckett had a close-up view of the political situation. More than a hundred newspapers circulated, including the popular anti-Semitic weekly *Völkischer Beobachter* and papers published by each of the Nazi leaders. By 1938, Goebbels had refined his paper as a "weapon of war," publishing unambiguous pronouncements that old scores from the inequitable Versailles Treaty of 1919 would be settled with buckets of blood. In 1937, it was punishable for visitors and citizens alike to possess a newspaper from any of twenty specified countries.[46]

As Beckett traveled from city to city, he observed the strict enforcement of the brutally severe anti-Semitic Nuremberg laws. When Beckett had left England, British sentiment toward Germany was complex and ambivalent, similar to that in many other countries. Support for appeasement or neutrality vied with sentiment for intervention. Hitler had been diabolical in playing individuals and nations like the French and British against each other. The issues at stake were support of Czechoslovakia and Spain versus the need to keep the peace. To Beckett, Hitler's intentions grew increasingly more obvious. He demanded the return of all pre–World War I German colonies and the cancellation of all reparation payments. He began increasing arms production and conscription. When he announced the actual pursuit of *lebensraum,* "living space," his intent to go to war was patent.

Sensing that war was imminent, Beckett left Germany.[47] Before making his final move to Paris, he stopped briefly in London and Dublin. In Dublin he testified against Oliver St. John Gogarty, charged with anti-Semitic defamation by his uncle's brother. Beckett began extensive research for a play about Dr. Johnson and Mrs. Thrale entitled *Human Wishes.* He also learned that on Herbert Read's recommendation (and after forty-two rejections), *Murphy* had been accepted for publication.[48]

Once settled in Paris, Beckett renewed his friendship with Joyce. On the night of January 7, 1938, an event occurred that has often been associated with Beckett's portrayals of the unfathomability of life. He was held up by a pimp, and when he resisted, the thief stabbed him in the chest, inflicting a near-fatal wound. Beckett subsequently asked his assailant why he had chosen him, and when the man replied, "Je ne sais pas, monsieur," Beckett did not press charges. Given the nature of the world he had been witnessing, Beckett may have felt that he had no special entitlement to freedom from attack or that random aggression was less evil than state-organized crime. The words "I don't know, Sir" are spoken by Godot's messengers in regard to the just nature of Godot.

During his subsequent two-week stay in the hospital he was visited regularly by Joyce and by Suzanne Deschevaux-Dumesnil, a pianist at the Paris Conservatoire. Suzanne later became Beckett's wife. In the fall of 1938, he and Suzanne moved into the seventh-floor apartment at 6 rue des Favorites that they would occupy until 1961. Here, Beckett wrote some poems that were published after the war and began translating *Murphy* into French with his friend Alfred Péron.[49]

The French press continued to detail world events: Hitler's overt pugnacity, the Japanese capture of Canton and Hankow, Mussolini's incorporation of Libya as a part of Italy, Franco's assault on Catalonia, and the ongoing Soviet purges. Headlines called attention to Germany's internal aggression against Jews, as exemplified by the rampages and massacre of Kristallnacht in November 1938, and its external threats against its neighbors.

Beckett owned and studied *Mein Kampf* in 1942. When he first read it, however, is uncertain;[50] the London *Times* had published excerpts in 1933, *Les Temps,* in 1938. Beckett did follow the events of the thirties, not just in London but in Germany and the rest of the world. Through his experiences during this terrible decade he gained a sense of the extraordinary cruelties people are capable of imposing on one another, whether through passive indifference or active deeds. "Was I sleeping while the others suffered?" he asks in *Waiting for Godot.* And Hamm in *Endgame* says, "You're on earth, there's no cure for that!"

Although Beckett did not see the full extent of the Nazi atrocities, his journey through Germany and subsequent world events as reported in the French press furnished him with images of incredible moral depredation. His firsthand experience of the Nazi regime was crucial in his swift decision to resist the German evil actively, rather than accept it passively, when Hitler's troops moved into Paris. Perhaps he thought, as Vladimir says in *Godot,* "Let us not waste our time in idle discourse! . . . Let us do something, while we have the chance! It is not everyday that we are needed. . . . At this place, at this moment of time, all mankind is us, whether we like it or not. . . . Let us represent worthily for once the foul brood to which a cruel fate consigned us!"

In November 1940, he joined Alfred Péron in the Resistance in Paris. In both occupied and unoccupied France, the expurgation of the Jews was escalating. At the same time, many organizations were printing anti-Nazi propaganda, and many action groups carried out sabotage activities. Beckett was one of the earliest to join in these resistance groups in 1940.

Beckett was always reluctant to discuss his war activities, but one can review them as they emerge out of the historical record of World War II.[51] His Paris group, Gloria, was funded by Special Operations Executive's (SOE) Prosper. (Winston Churchill's SOE oversaw all underground activities in the occupied nations, and its only requirements were that its non-French agents speak impeccable French and have a thorough knowledge of French culture.) The Resistance scholar Henri Michel reports that Gloria, like the other small circuits, retained its autonomy and conducted business as it wished.[52] The same independence was true of Etoile, another group with which Beckett was associated. All the same, as M. R. D. Foot reports, Gloria, again like the other small circuits, looked to Prosper's leaders, François Suttill, a poet, and Armel Guerne, a translator, for arms and supplies. Although the leaders met regularly with resisters at a black market restaurant near the Arc de Triomphe and at a café near Sacre-Coeur, "some of Guerne's intellectuals, like Samuel Beckett," had the "intelligence and the security sense" to lie low.[53]

Beckett's specific assignments with Gloria at first involved collecting information, sometimes in code, regarding German troop movements, which he deciphered, classified, and typed before it was smuggled out to London; later on, he transferred the information to microfilm. In August, after one of Gloria's members was tortured until he confessed, Beckett's friend Péron was arrested, and the rest of the group faced imminent exposure; only thirty of eighty survived in the end. At 11 A.M. on August 15, Péron's wife sent Suzanne and Beckett a telegram, telling them to leave Paris immediately. By 3 P.M., they were gone, traveling mostly on foot and at night toward Roussillon, in the unoccupied zone in the south. Jack MacGowran speaks of Beckett in flight as a "key man" for whom Nazi bullets were marked.[54]

Once in Roussillon, Beckett's clandestine activities included setting up contacts between Resistance workers and the pickup, hiding, and delivering of ammunition for the destruction of railroad yards used in transporting German supplies. By the time Beckett arrived in Roussillon, the Germans had invaded the unoccupied zone; all native and foreign-born Jews not in hiding were routinely picked up and killed or deported. The Germans intensified their recruitment of French males for their factories, with the result that more and more young men joined the maquis. By this time, anyone suspected of any kind of underground activity faced grave danger.

Roussillon served Beckett well, as one learns from the extensive research of the French cultural historian Laurence Wylie, whose study of Roussillon allows one to fill in some of Beckett's dramatically different day- and nighttime activities during the last two and a half years of the war.[55] Wylie describes the village of Roussillon as a natural hideout for someone on the run. Thirty-five miles from Avignon, it was accessible only by car or bike. Even before the war, the area was known as an escape from civilization.[56] During the war, it became a refuge for many escaping the German conscription law. As such, it became a natural home for the growing number of maquis, especially during 1943–44.

Survival in Roussillon was not difficult. Although Beckett rented a house (still referred to as "la maison Beckett") next to the local leader of the maquis, free housing was readily available. Because the town's population had shrunk from 1,600 to 779, many of the older houses were unoccupied and unowned. The old deserted windmills also sheltered refugees, and for fast concealment the many abandoned quarries in the cliffs had entries marked by black holes left from stone erosion. One could raise goats for milk and cheese, harvest grain for bread, and cultivate the local berries for fruit and jelly. Beckett worked as a farmer.

The villagers welcomed Beckett as they had the many other refugees who settled there. His keen awareness that he was an Irishman-become-Parisian resistance agent, whose circuit had been exposed—a targeted man in hiding—may explain his odd registration at the town hall as Samuel Beckett from Dublin, England. But the wife of Beckett's painter-friend Henri Hayden, also in Roussillon, makes clear that the villagers were no more suspicious of him than of one another.[57] They had a deep sense of privacy and had no idea of Beckett's recent past; they grew to like this new member of their community. Furthermore, she explains of Beckett's work in the fields, "he [labored] out of friendship with the peasants."[58]

It seems inconceivable that Beckett would not have feared exposure, but all reports point to the contrary.[59] He welcomed structured activity like a job in Roussillon's shrinking war and black-market economy or any physical activity to make his days meaningful. He loved the open country and frequently walked long distances. The village's sparse mountainous areas, extraordinarily clear air, and remarkable ruins, windmills, and quarries reminded him of his childhood Ireland.

Resistance activity at night gave purpose to his life, as did his writing. He wrote *Watt* during these years, which acted as a kind of healing process, as he put it, "to get away from war and occupation." It was a means of "staying sane."[60] Beckett came to share what Wylie calls the villagers' strong sense of survival, of "*d'broussillement*" or "*système d-*," that is, their stoical accommodation to whatever was required of them to endure.[61] Pursuing life as usual during war, this *système d-* was another important model in Beckett's growing affirmation of human durability.

To be sure, the townspeople knew the maquis were everywhere, settling old accounts with friends and enemies but blaming the Germans and Vichy. If they were organized, it was as much through the friendship system as through the Fighting French or SOE. Resistance activity continued in nearby Apt, Saint Saturnin, and Goult as well, but the center of maquis activity was in Gordes, five kilometers away. On one occasion, after tracing the maquis to Gordes, the Germans brought tanks and artillery to a hilltop and opened fire, destroying many houses and a large part of the terrain. This event, like the loud denunciations and public executions in Saint Saturnin, did not overtly concern the Roussillians, who looked the other way. Most knew that one Alsatian in their midst was maquis, as was Beckett's next-door neighbor and another who adopted numerous orphans. During the day, these maquisards pursued their lives of habit and family responsibility; at night, they arranged private rendezvous. The townspeople did not live in a state of fear because they were scattered and, more important, because they had a prosperous, caring Vichy mayor who was committed to keeping things quiet. Numerous Roussillon maquis victories are on record.[62]

Interestingly, Foot attributes the inspiration of the Resistance throughout Europe to a person still "within living memory": Michael Collins, military chief of the Irish Republican Army during the troubles of 1916–22. To Foot, Collins was the greatest resistance leader of the century. He understood the tactics of what he called irregular warfare and the basic grammar of sabotage. The Irish resistance under Collins during 1916–21 was, in Foot's opinion, comparable to France in 1939–45.[63] Although Foot admits that not many Europeans would have heard of Collins and thus associated the French and Irish situations, Beckett surely would have done so.

Beckett dismissed his World War II activities as "boy-scout stuff," a typically modest response, but he was one of very few to join the Resistance as early as 1940. And when he later took refuge in Roussillon, rather than cower in hiding, he fought with the maquis. Following the war, he was decorated by Charles de Gaulle with the Croix de Guerre for his "distinguished noncombatant activities." Beckett's medal, with a silver star, indicates specific acts of bravery "in divisional despatch." The phrase suggests an alignment with a fighting unit, such as the French Forces of the Interior, which had, by that time, amalgamated members of the SOE, Resistance, and Maquis.[64] He also received the Médaille de la Résistance. To both of these honors, he responded with typical reserve and humility.

Alec Reid remarks of Beckett's early involvement with the Resistance, "[He] took no active part in affairs until the Germans occupied Paris. . . . Then the war suddenly became something personal and with meaning. Like Joyce, Beckett had many Jewish friends and he was incensed by the constant humiliations and maltreatments to which they were subjected. He was enraged too at the repeated shootings by the Germans of innocent people taken as hostages. . . . He couldn't stand with his arms folded."[65] Beckett may have seemed apolitical in the traditional sense of the term, but he had powerful convictions regarding his moral obligations to others. He could not accept the evil imposition of suffering on others with his "arms folded," whatever the personal risk. The war further enabled Beckett to engage in activities requiring the kind of courage of which his father and uncles would have been proud. It allowed him an arena in which to activate those values he had always deeply held. And if, in the passage of these terrible years, he despaired over the unjust deaths of friends and acquaintances, his activities allowed him an outlet in which to pursue a kind of justice for them.

As a man of exquisite feeling and introspection, and as a survivor, Beckett, I believe, by 1940, was able to balance the events of his life, as one juggles art and life, experience and ideology. In the process of maturing and separating from a well loved and loving family, he rejected his family's Victorian values of financial security and traditional marriage, while he retained their fundamental commitment to virtue. He developed close associations with others who shared his high sense of moral integrity and who encouraged his independence and artistic pursuits.

The war and its aftermath gave Beckett an opportunity to become his own person: to practice, if you will, the moral ideals he had been taught at home and school and thus to integrate the values of his childhood and adulthood. The war was an opportunity to confront, not merely contemplate, matters of human will, moral choice, and good and evil. Beckett had long been a devoted student of philosophy, but for the remainder of his life he maintained that he was no philosopher—and one should probably take him at his word. He never reached the certainties of Plato, Aristotle, the stoics, Kant, or even his contemporaries Camus and Sartre. Neither did he demonstrate the kind of religious faith that had moved other resisters. Beckett had, nevertheless, demonstrated the highest values of moral commitment. If, as the philosophers had taught him, virtue is dependent upon character and action, rather than being the product of an a priori state of being or "meaning," then Beckett's actions throughout the war were exemplary. Although under no immediate threat himself, Beckett repeatedly put his life in danger to battle the enemies of human decency.

Furthermore, fighting an enemy of uncontested and categorical evil enabled Beckett to respond to a pain that he had carried since childhood, namely, the experience of Ireland's Civil War, which introduced him at an early age to the depths of human suffering. As he told more than one person, he never forgot the day in 1916 when he saw O'Connell Street in flames. Now, in 1940, he would witness another nation torn from within: French fighting French as the Resistance opposed the Vichy collaborators, just as in Ireland, twenty-five years earlier, he had seen kinsmen fighting kinsmen. At the end of the war, when the maquis marched in victory through Roussillon, "there stood Beckett at the front of the procession, carrying the flag."[66] One can only imagine the pride and relief that prompted such a rare gesture of public display. But given the complexity of the times and the man and the lessons he had learned about potential good and evil in human nature, he remained, thereafter, entirely modest about the war. His nephew, Edward Beckett, reports that his uncle never spoke about his wartime experiences except in very general terms.[67]

In May 1945, Beckett returned to Ireland. He had not seen his family in five years. He intended to return to Paris, where Suzanne awaited him, but restrictions had been placed on resident aliens owing to severe shortages in France. Beckett then volunteered to help build a hospital in Saint-Lô, a project arranged by both the Irish and French Red Cross. Only after this did he return to his apartment and begin his "siege in the room," the prodigious outpouring of work for which he was to achieve an international reputation.

The same altruistic impulses that had motivated Beckett's earlier Resistance activities prompted him to join the ranks in Saint-Lô. Although he performed the most menial and boring of tasks, everything he did was in the service of rebuilding and healing. Saint-Lô gave Beckett the opportunity to continue his previous activities in the service of humanity, a logical extension and perhaps a consummation of his prewar and war experiences. Beckett was determined to battle suffering, whether this involved combating an evil invading force or alleviating the destruction caused by friendly fire.

He would now become a healer, an active participant in the restoration of one of the postwar ruins of the world. He would again wear the uniform of the medical assistant, the orderly's dress, which he had worn more than ten years before when he worked at the mental hospital in London. Indeed, at this time in history, the world might well have seemed a madhouse without walls. In addition, as a onetime Irish exile now working with an Irish group in France, Beckett could connect his past with the nation that was to become his future, permanent home.

The Allied invasion of Saint-Lô was "possibly the most momentous epoch in [humanity's] annals."[68] The once-beautiful Saint-Lô, now a grotesque funeral pyre, was a charred and broken world, every landmark transmuted into ash. The Saint-Lois had illustrated the combination of human misery and human resilience—the absurd victory—that Beckett would shortly write about. The townspeople had achieved liberation through unspeakable suffering. They had sustained the bizarre paradox of a relatively peaceful, if humiliating, enemy occupation, followed by a destructive, if liberating, victory. Gratitude at salvation, freedom gained at the cost of incomprehensible despair, would be an ingredient of Beckett's future tragicomedy: a gloss, perhaps, on Lucky's lucky relationship to the brutal Pozzo in *Godot*.

Ultimately, Beckett's experience in Saint-Lô provided him with a long-awaited equanimity, in a larger, metaphysical sense. It gave him a sense of balance, of what in *Godot* he would call the tears and laughter of the world—the black-comic alternation of elation and despair that is the individual's lot, as well as the nature of history.

Stephen Dedalus in *A Portrait of the Artist as a Young Man* defines Aristotle's pity in tragic emotion as "the feeling which arrests the mind in the presence of whatsoever is grave and constant in human sufferings and unites it with the human sufferer." He then defines the accompanying fear in tragic emotion as "the feeling which arrests the mind in the presence of whatsoever is grave and constant in human sufferings and unites it with the secret cause." Joyce's distinction between pity for the "sufferer" and fear for the "cause" might well have been the terms of reference with which Beckett long identified. But in Saint-Lô, I suggest, he witnessed a living example of the human capacity both for destructiveness and for stoical forbearance, courage, humanity, and even humor in the face of brutal forces. It must also have stirred resonances within him of what he had first seen as a youth in Dublin and Belfast and later, as an adult, in London, Germany, and wartime France.

Beckett arrived in Saint-Lô at the beginning of the construction project. The workers were to build one hundred makeshift wooden huts to be used for hospital facilities; they would plant flowers and trees. The patients were survivors of bombings and concentration camps, and all suffered from tuberculosis and the diseases of wartime.

When the supplies arrived—174 tons of equipment, including six ambulances, a utility wagon and lorry, and medications like penicillin and blood serum—Beckett's first tasks included picking them up; he also drove staff to and from various destinations and did whatever was called for. He performed all his duties with enthusiasm and generosity. He met new arrivals from Ireland in Dieppe in his large Ford V-8 utility wagon and drove them to Saint-Lô; he greeted them with enormous bags of plums, grapes, and pears.

When more supplies arrived, Beckett worked alongside both local laborers and the one thousand German POWs on loan from the French government; in fact, he wore the same uniform the prisoners did. They sorted, stacked, and made stock cards for the 250 tons of supplies that had arrived. Beckett's activities in Saint-Lô, as described by those who worked with him, attest to those attributes that became associated with him for the rest of his life: generosity, kindness, a sense of responsibility, and modesty. Jim Gaffney, an attending physician, described Beckett's general caring and good nature: "[Beckett] is a most valuable asset to the unit—terribly conscientious about his work and enthusiastic about the future of the hospital; [he] like[s] a game of bridge and in every way [is] a most likeable chap, aged abut [sic] 38–40, [of] no religious persuasion; I should say a free thinker—but he pounced on a little rosary beads which was on a stall in Notre Dame to bring back as a little present to Tommy D. It was very thoughtful of him."[69]

After Beckett returned to Paris, his great creative siege began. He wrote the radio speech "The Capital of the Ruins" (June 10, 1946), occasioned by Dublin press coverage of France's ostensible lack of appreciation of the Irish effort in Saint-Lô.[70] Beckett's intention, clearly reconciliatory, was to praise both the French and Irish. His decision to make a public statement, however, exceptional for this man, and the nature of that statement deserve close inspection, for Beckett is atypically explicit in his personal and philosophical reflections. We know in retrospect that the end of the war marked a major turning point in his life. In this speech, Beckett went beyond the Saint-Lô experience to express a vision derived from his entire life thus far. He would later say that he wrote from impotence and ignorance, but there is a sense here of his wisdom and self-confidence. Perhaps for just this moment Beckett experienced a sense of knowing and a conviction of his own courage. Perhaps these were to be the foundation for his retreat to the room, during which he engaged the world of his imagination. Beckett was forty when he wrote the speech.

In this beautiful and moving statement, Beckett exalts both the comfort to be drawn from the inward human capacity to surmount circumstances of the utmost gravity and the sustenance to be given and gained in moments of camaraderie. In addition, he sets forth several articles of faith that will resonate throughout his great works to come. The first is his awareness of the human capacity to endure the caprices of circumstance: "What was important was not our having penicillin . . . [but] the occasional glimpse obtained, by us in them [the patients] and, who knows, by them in us . . . of that smile at the human condition as little to be extinguished by bombs as to be broadened by the elixirs of Burroughes and Welcome, the smile deriding, among other things, the having and not having, the giving and the taking, sickness and health." The "smile deriding . . . the having and not having" would become, in *Waiting for Godot,* that which enables humanity to face the fact that "the tears of the world are a constant quantity." The smile also enables the consolation one derives from the corollary truth: "The same is true of the laugh."

Beckett's second point seems to be that while the material universe is provisional and ephemeral, acts of mundane generosity are not: "The hospital of wooden huts and its gardens between the Vire and Bayeux roads will continue to discharge its function, and its cured. 'Provisional' is not the term it was in this universe become provisional. It will continue to discharge its function long after the Irish are gone." Beckett seems to be extolling the human impulse to give of oneself to the suffering. It is this that is a steadfast thread in the human fabric, an aspect of life that is not provisional. Implicit in this remark is Beckett's contrast between the abiding nature of the human spirit and the transitory trappings of worldly power, between the permanence of generosity and the impermanent edifices of the material world. Also implicit here is his faith, as he again writes in *Waiting for Godot,* that regardless of circumstance, humanity will "represent worthily the foul brood to which a cruel fate consigned us."

In perhaps his most optimistic statement, Beckett declares that the act of giving uplifts the giver as well as the recipient: "Those who were in Saint-Lô will come home realising that they got at least as good as they gave." This may be our salvation as we await Godot.

Beckett would proceed to evoke artistically increasingly sparse human habitations, and his worlds and its figures would seem to pale in comparison with, say, Joyce's grand invocations of human possibility. But Beckett, perhaps more so than Joyce, had come to understand the limitations imposed upon the individual by powerful and eternally unpredictable inner and outer forces—that is, the limits posed by the absurdity of the human condition. In this remarkable radio speech, Beckett defines what we will come to intuit in his later work as life's redeeming virtues. The individual's fate may be provisional and the course of history may be provisional, but the smile that derides the conditional is not. Its source is in the human spirit, and from this come healers of a moment: those who build hospitals, those who dance a jig, and those who would entertain a reader. The hospitals, like the dancers and the names of fictional characters, will fade, just as the names of the ordinary Irish and French patriots will be forgotten—but the spirit that moves them will not.

Finally, as a man of specific place and origin—always rooted in this world and certainly not an artist-would-be-god or an unworldly aesthete—Beckett stresses that the Irish in Saint-Lô demonstrated the best part of human nature, that quality that seeks not to dominate or desolate but rather to heal and console. With evident Irish pride he adds, "I think that to the end of its hospital days, it will be called the Irish Hospital, and after that the huts, when they have been turned into dwellings, the Irish huts."

At the end of the speech, revealing what was perhaps for him the crucial wisdom that would direct his future work, he adds, "I may perhaps venture to mention another [possibility], more remote but perhaps of greater import . . . the possibility that *[those in Saint-Lô] . . . got indeed what they could hardly give, a vision and sense of a time-honoured concept of humanity in ruins, and perhaps even an inkling of the terms in which our condition is to be thought again.* These will have been in France" (emphasis added). The willingness to give of oneself to the suffering is not only an abiding part of human nature. It is also the very means through which one can gain an "inkling" of the mystery of the human condition.

When Beckett wrote this speech, he had already resigned his post at Saint-Lô and was settled in Paris. The speech was thus one of his earliest postwar writings. Indeed, his earlier remark about the endurance of the Irish spirit and his final reminder that these lessons will have been consummated in France reconcile the land of his origin with the land of his destiny. In addressing "our condition . . . to be thought again," Beckett braced himself for the great creative task now facing him. *Waiting for Godot* would follow shortly.

TWO

Waiting for Godot: The Existential Dimension

VLADIMIR: All I know is that the hours are long, under these conditions, and constrain us to beguile them with proceedings which—how shall I say—which may at first sight seem reasonable, until they become a habit. You may say it is to prevent our reason from foundering. No doubt. But has it not long been straying in the night without end of the abyssal depths? That's what I sometimes wonder. You follow my reasoning?

ESTRAGON: . . . We are all born mad. Some remain so.

Waiting for Godot

Though human affairs are not worthy of great seriousness, it is yet necessary to be serious. . . . God alone is worthy of supreme seriousness, but man is God's plaything. . . . What then is the right way of living? Life must be lived as play, playing certain games, making sacrifices, singing and dancing, and then a man will be able to propitiate the gods, and defend himself against his enemies, and win in the contest.

Johan Huizinga

In a world devoid of belief systems, the mind and heart cry out for validation, for the assurance that life has meaning and actions have purpose. One may accept, as an existential truth, the assumption that despite the individual's endeavors to comprehend or change the world, "there is no new thing under the sun" (Ecclesiastes), and, as Beckett puts it, "the tears of the world are a constant quantity. . . ." But one also occupies a world of temporal measurement. Time passes and one ages, and, facing these inescapable facts, one journeys with tenacious will through the arbitrary divisions of time and space holding onto goals and belief systems as if they were absolute.

Life is not what the traditional dramatists portrayed, a series of ordered events with beginnings, middles, and ends. Neither are language and logic effective means for the communication and discernment of meaning. Nevertheless, the human creature, even if no longer motivated by the conviction of a divine mission, is continuously compelled toward purposeful activity. The need for a moral or spiritual anchor remains.

Waiting for Godot portrays both the need for purpose and the emotional fragmentation that accompanies the struggle for this anchoring of self. Vladimir and Estragon have inherited a world they cannot master, and despite their heroic accommodations they cannot escape the turmoil that accompanies their sense of purposelessness. It is as though an unfathomable anarchy had been loosed upon their inner world. Most of their efforts toward filling this emptiness reinforce their loss of energy and indecision and increase the disjuncture between their thoughts and actions. In reality, they are capable of participating only in temporarily meaningful action and fragmented communication. And they know this.

That they persist defines their courage; during their good moments they explain:

ESTRAGON: I wasn't doing anything.

VLADIMIR: Perhaps you weren't. But it's the way of doing it that counts, the way of doing it, if you want to go on living.

ESTRAGON: I wasn't doing anything.

VLADIMIR: You must be happy too, deep down. . . .

ESTRAGON: Would you say so? . . .
VLADIMIR: Say, I am happy.
ESTRAGON: I am happy.
VLADIMIR: So am I.

. . .

ESTRAGON: So am I. . . .
VLADIMIR: Wait . . . we embraced. . . . We were happy . . . happy. What do we do now that we're happy . . . Go on waiting . . . waiting.

During their worst moments, boredom and ambivalence are replaced by anxiety and mutual intimidation: "There are times when I wonder if it wouldn't be better for us to part." Having searched the world for role models, for anything that might inspire a sense of purpose (and their conversations are filled with the wisdom of the ages), their quest remains unfulfilled. If their past has provided no codes or figures to respect or emulate, their future is similarly disheartening. They will inspire no disciples, peers, or children, for if they lack a coherent belief structure and sense of self, what legacy could they offer anyone else? Their repeated inability to act—" 'Let's go.' *(They do not move.)*"—reflects their deepest awareness of their failed efforts to discern anything right or purposeful in life. In order to act, after all, one needs a sense of direction, of ideals or goals.

The paradox of survival in *Waiting for Godot* involves a rereading of Camus' "The Myth of Sisyphus." Sisyphus had the choice of abandoning his rock at the foot of the mountain or of continuously rolling it to the top, the only certainty being that after the rock fell, he could, if he so chose, once more perform this arduous, useless act. For Camus, Sisyphus's perseverance, in literal spite or contempt of the meaninglessness of his task, defined his superiority. By ignoring the irrationality of his fate and focusing on the blue of the sky and the texture of the rock, he could exult in his defiance of fate.

The paradox of Camus' Absurdism, like Sartre's Existentialism, demands a tension between engagement and impotence and between logic and absurdity, where the awareness of life's ultimate meaninglessness—*when placed at the recesses of the mind*—allows one to live fully and without anguish in a random and disordered universe. But Beckett's heroes differ from those of Camus: they lack a sense of defiance regarding their lot in life. One would never imagine a weary, disconsolate Sisyphus at the end of his rope, either literally or metaphorically; but this is Vladimir and Estragon's frequent situation.

Beckett's people also lack Sisyphus's most minimal assurances, for example, that the rock or the mountain will be present the next day or that time and space are as they appear. It is not only dubious as to whether Beckett's characters' most modest wishes can be fulfilled, but it is unclear if what they speak or hear is the intended message. They lack the most basic certainties upon which defiance depends, and this, along with their voluntary submersion of individual identity in role playing as a means of survival, makes them aliens in Sisyphus's world. The word *happiness,* used by Camus to finally describe Sisyphus, is, at best, only occasionally applicable to Beckett's figures.

Vladimir and Estragon's only certainty is the terrible uncertainty of the world, together with their accompanying need to assume that somehow and someday meaning will become manifest. That there must be a Godot who will provide this is the ultimate focus of their everyday activities, and in their pursuit of this hope lies the paradox of their busyness in waiting.

The very act of survival or waiting becomes Beckett's exposition of the games and rituals people construct in order to pass the hours and years, the accommodations they make to those closest in their lives, the alternation of hope and despair they endure in these accommodations, and the illusions and rejections of illusion that accompany each of these acts. Vladimir and Estragon's relationship is thus geared to distract them from boredom, to lift depression, and to fight paralysis. Although there are many other ways of surviving a world bereft of meaning, including work, family life, and social action, they have rejected these alternatives, despite scattered evidence in the play that they were onetime considerations. Vladimir and Estragon have also rejected the more self-indulgent roles that permit the outlet of anger and frustration, those less salutary emotions that accompany one's experience of the void. Masters like Pozzo and servants like Lucky pursue these less admirable roles, of the dictatorial sadist and submissive masochist; even for them, as Pozzo admits, "the road seems long when one journeys all alone." But Vladimir and Estragon assume a more humane relationship, one in which Vladimir assumes the more rational, philosophical role and Estragon the emotional, instinctual one; by so doing they can aspire to some egalitarian stability. They may pursue a relatively peaceful and predictable coexistence, unless, of course, something out of the ordinary disrupts their equanimity, something such as the intrusion of strangers like Lucky and Pozzo. Should this occur, as it does, their masks will fragment, and their less savory aspects will surface and rupture the equilibrium of their relationship.

The existential condition thus establishes the philosophical backdrop of the play, although Beckett neither answers nor systematically interrogates theoretical issues. It is in Beckett's rich depiction of both conscious and unconscious thought, the subject of future chapters, that *Godot* achieves its great intensity. That is, equally exposed in his characters' survival games is the emotional landscape in which their stratagems for survival function. This Beckett accomplishes by counterpointing the activities and efforts to manage each day with the feeling of emptiness and loneliness that motivates the well-patterned scenarios. Repeated objects, phrases, literary references, gestures, and spatial patterns—the mise-en-scène—become manifestations of the masked emotional life. In his emerging poetic images of hopelessness and despair, Beckett reveals the inner mind in counterpoint to the conscious efforts to survive. Dramatic conflict depends upon revelations about human nature within the context of the human condition.

First, Vladimir and Estragon appear as agents of free will; regardless of their doubts and despair about the future, they choose to live rather than the alternative. Unlike Camus' solitary Sisyphus, Beckett's journeymen have a companion for comfort or distraction; this may give them a better chance of surviving. But this is a complicated arrangement, for if their existential needs and emotional hunger necessitate their interdependence, defined by specific role play, these constructs betray them as well. Emotional needs continuously surface, and because role playing is, after all, an arbitrary accommodation to the mess, the most carefully patterned script may produce identity confusion and role reversals; at times, the scripts may fail completely. The plays's most compelling moments occur when an authenticity of self emerges. Ultimately, the insoluble problem is that each player has needs that will forever be unmet: Vladimir will never have anyone to answer his philosophical inquiries, just as Estragon will never have anyone to listen to his dreams. Thus, they await Godot, unsure of who or what "he" is and entirely unsure of the outcome of their awaited meeting. They are not disheartened over the possibility that Godot may be a brute: they know, after all, that Godot beats the young messenger boy, yet they still wait. It would be worthwhile if he came, even if he abused them, so intense is their need for direction.

Godot, then, is that someone or something that would obviate the need for the games that tentatively provide a purpose in life. Waiting is the human condition, in which one constructs games or a lifestyle that mask the unknowable. The name of Vladimir and Estragon's game is "To be or not to be," and when they whisper or weep over this question, their words resound in a void reminiscent of Ecclesiastes: "Vanity of vanities; all is vanity." That their deepest dimensions of being prohibit any sense of peace recalls Hamlet's "I could be bounded in a nutshell, and count myself a king of infinite space, were it not that I have bad dreams." Confronted with such complex stage images, we, the audience, engage *Waiting for Godot* with responses much like those of Vladimir and Estragon. As we progress through the time of the play, we too await a denouement, an intuition of meaning, Godot.

STAGING THE EXISTENTIAL

Waiting for Godot encompasses a sparse natural world—of animal (man), mineral (the road and Estragon's mound or rock), and vegetable (Vladimir's tree). Its two inhabitants perform the most basic functions: one or the other eats, sleeps, urinates, exercises, dances, embraces the other, argues, or sulks. They also think. Within the mysterious cycles of external nature (a radish displacing a carrot) there seem to be intimations of a larger, equally mysterious cosmic world (an unpredictable moon). In comprehending the natural or supernatural, as the play's first line announces, there would seem to be "Nothing to be done."

Lacking a social history or identity, *Godot*'s Everymen are being, or existence without essence. They stand before us asking to be understood, as they themselves try to understand, and they exist, as we respond to them, in a context of virtual absence and its correlative, endless potentiality. Standing on a road that similarly lacks definition in that it goes toward and has descended from nowhere, they define themselves primarily in their relationship to one other and with roles so well scripted that each is the other's audience: each gives validation to the other's existence. Simultaneously, even while adhering to a script, each is the main actor in the scenario that plays out his life. That Vladimir and Estragon share the singularly most profound life goal, that is, of determining a purpose for living, is clear in the very name of their quest: Godot. If this refers to (a diminutive) God, the external world (cosmic or natural) might provide their much-needed rootedness. But Godot is also virtually a contraction of their nicknames, Gogo and Didi, the inner self that might alternatively give cohesion to their lives. As Gogo and Didi thus await an answer, an external or internal solution, it is natural, in moments of disorientation or disconnection, when they say, "Let's go" that they also return to their game with the ritualistic "We're waiting for Godot."

The universe in which they function reflects their identities and is a construct of how they envision it. The archetypal tree, rock, and lonely road lend themselves to multiple associations, some of which are ironic. The rock is not Sisyphean or Promethean; it is merely a place to sit; the tree, first skeletal and later blossoming, neither permits them a place to hang or crucify themselves in an effort to emulate the absent deity or simply to escape their failed lives; nor does it fulfill its function as the designated meeting place with Godot. The leaves of the tree, an ambiguous sign of regeneration or hope, become a symphony of voices that haunts them with elegies of past sojourners who similarly walked this lonely road. The most minimal objects in their possession recall other echoes of the historic and mythic past—all consumed with the question "To be or not to be?" To live is to think, and to think embraces all the voices of the silence. Peace or, more precisely, silence, as Beckett himself once stated, may be attained only in death.

Beckett mirrors the paradoxes of existentialism—the persistent need to act on precariously grounded stages—with the repeated absence of denouement in the enacted scenarios. Since much of act I, with its series of miniplays, is repeated in the second act, which concludes with an implicit return to act I, Beckett creates a never-ending series of incomplete plays within the larger drama, each of which lacks a resolving deus ex machina.

The paradox of purposive action and ultimate meaninglessness pervades. A deceptively simple boot routine is rationalized as purposeful activity:

VLADIMIR: It'd pass the time.
(Estragon hesitates.)
I assure you, it'd be an occupation.
ESTRAGON: A relaxation.

VLADIMIR: A recreation.
ESTRAGON: A relaxation. . . . We don't manage too badly, eh Didi, between the two of us? . . . We always find something, eh Didi, to give us the impression we exist.

At times, their stoicism weakens. Routines fail to disguise the anguish of feeling (in Estragon) or of thinking (in Vladimir). Vladimir entreats Estragon to play his part: "Come on, Gogo, return the ball, can't you . . . ?" Estragon must similarly encourage Vladimir: "That's the idea, let's make a little conversation." At some points, the couple finds it difficult to distract each other from "seeking," which implies the act of "finding" (there is "nothing to be found"), which would inevitably lead back to "thinking," which is, as they say, "the worst." Then, their exchanges, with multiple overtones from the Crucifixion to the Holocaust, follow:

ESTRAGON: The best thing would be to kill me, like the other.
VLADIMIR: What other? . . .
ESTRAGON: Like billions of others.
VLADIMIR: *(sententious)* To every man his little cross. . . . Where are all these corpses from?
ESTRAGON: These skeletons . . .
VLADIMIR: A charnel-house! A charnel-house!
ESTRAGON: You don't have to look.
VLADIMIR: You can't help looking.
ESTRAGON: True.

Perhaps, they meditate, it might be best to just "hear" ("We are incapable of keeping silent"), although hearing brings back the voices of the leaves, their thoughts, and the past, whereupon they are thrust into the circular miasma of thought-frustration-rationalization. Their goal remains the ambitious: "to try to converse calmly" according to their well-performed script:

ESTRAGON: So long as one knows.
VLADIMIR: One can bide one's time.
ESTRAGON: One knows what to expect.
VLADIMIR: No further need to worry.
ESTRAGON: Simply wait.
VLADIMIR: We're used to it.

At times, they reveal the true subject of their game:

VLADIMIR: Now what did we do yesterday? . . .
ESTRAGON: Yesterday evening we spent blathering about *nothing*. (emphasis added)

Even if these well-planned interchanges fail to adequately anesthetize them, there are workable alternatives. They can play with their words: "Calm . . . cawm," "tray bong"; poke fun at, contradict, or create versions of their generic script: "That's the idea, let's contradict ourselves. . . . This is becoming really meaningless." Then their words can become like their hats, to be juggled to fill the void, another means of diffusing anxiety. As for their words as communicative tools, Vladimir and Estragon learned long ago that words not only are inadequate constructs for authentic experience but that, at best, they connect on different and variable wavelengths. The permutations and combinations regarding meaning are legion.

But Vladimir and Estragon remain exemplary in the elasticity of their absurd accommodation. Among their adversaries—the unknown, erratic, or uncontrollable forces—is logic, which appears to be more discrete and manageable than, say, such fateful events as physical debilitation or the sudden appearance of intruding strangers or any occurrence that might change their routine. Logic, after all, gives the impression of cohesion and viability. It seduces one toward feats of accomplishment; it helps in the pursuit of survival. It dictates coherence, indicating this, rather than that, course of action.

It also gives one a sense of comfort, for it is a natural state of mind. And thus, Vladimir and Estragon's most ordinary routines, even their silliest vaudeville exchanges, like the bowler hat jostling, depend on the mechanics of logic, on continuity and causality. In fact, most of their interchanges depend on memory, which again depends on continuity and causality. If their games fail, they have emergency measures, which depend upon their past knowledge of one another and their anticipation of the other's response. Although a good deal of *Godot*'s humor arises from the two men's failure to enact simple tasks, like removing shoes and buttoning pants, and while habit may be a "great deadener" of anxiety, habit continues to demonstrate one's logic in a random and chaotic universe and provides the hope of linear and predictable behavior. As such, the characters insist on the truth or validity of their actions. Vladimir insists, "That's right," and when speaking of the limited human condition and need to help others, says, "It is true . . . we are no less a credit to our species." Lucky also asserts that the content of his monologue is "established beyond all doubt," although Pozzo insists there is not a "word of truth" in a remark made to him. Vladimir similarly implores the messenger to tell them the truth, and because they receive the answer they expect, they grow more confused about their query than before they asked it. Even Vladimir, Beckett's logician, concludes his seemingly lucid "Was I sleeping?" speech by wondering: "But in all that what truth will there be?" Vladimir and Estragon's major logical problem is why their designated appointment with Godot never materializes.

Ultimately, Vladimir and Estragon doubt; therefore they exist, and in their most modest, mutually willed activities, just as in their responses to the gratuitous events that befall them, they are pawns of an undefined fate that determines the erratic efficacy of causality and any of logic's other manifestations.

Sensory experience is another adversary and dimension in the absurdist paradox. One would assume that, like logic, sense perception is natural and reliable. Yet when Estragon asks for a carrot and is given a turnip, Vladimir says, "Oh pardon! I could have sworn it was a carrot." Their most facile assumptions regarding the simplest of sense perceptions are uncertain: although Estragon is traditionally portrayed as the portlier of the two men, their conversation about the rope that might hang them suggests the reverse:

ESTRAGON: Gogo light—bough not break—Gogo dead. Didi heavy—bough break—Didi alone. . . .
VLADIMIR: But am I heavier than you?
ESTRAGON: So you tell me. I don't know. There's an even chance. Or nearly.

The reality of human incapacity is nowhere more evident than in their use of language. The inability of words to communicate the most urgent of situations is underscored when each man cries for help and is treated much as though he had asked for the time of day. "Help me!" elicits the response, "It hurts?" So, too, even if language, logic, and the senses appear to hold, and the two try to assert their will, as Vladimir explains, one is not master of his moods. Thus, contradictions of word and mood are frequent, such as, "*Vladimir:* Don't touch me! Don't question me! Don't speak to me! Stay with me!" and "*Estragon:* I missed you . . . and at the same time I was happy."

Finally, there is time, the least comprehensible of their adversaries and perhaps the most terrifying. Despite their every effort, Vladimir and Estragon cannot deal with either mechanical or cosmic time. They can change neither themselves nor the world, which operates independently of them. To change would necessitate a sense of purpose, but because the world is indifferent in providing this, Vladimir and Estragon know well one of Beckett's axiomatic truths: In the absence of attainable goals or ideals, nothing, in a concrete way, *can* change. As Martin Esslin, who understood Beckett's sense of time, explains, "Waiting is to experience the action of time, which is constant change. And yet, as nothing real ever happens, that change in itself is an illusion. The ceaseless activity of time is self-defeating, purposeless, and therefore null and void. The more things change, the more they are the same. That is the terrible stability of the world."[1] Nevertheless, Beckett's play appears to move in a linear manner toward the future when Godot will arrive; and it is filled with traditional terms like *tomorrow* and *yesterday* and the colloquial exaggeration *a million years ago* and specifics like *in the nineties.* These, however, appropriately in an existential universe, function either in personal or in abstract terms. That is, in *Godot,* days, months, and even years pass in an instant; the tree blooms overnight; in what they believe is the next day, Pozzo and Lucky age; Pozzo is blind, Lucky, dumb. "When! When!" laments Pozzo. "Have you not done tormenting me with your accursed time?" Beckett's figures live out their lives before us existentially, and in their recurrent identification with historical and biblical figures they become archetypes of all humanity.

Time thus bends and contracts throughout *Godot,* as Beckett constructs a multidimensional tapestry of the human condition. One plays out one's life against a complex counterpoint of mechanical time (in which one ages and moves to death and obliteration), and cosmic time (in which one's acts have no function whatsoever). In the end, one's life is enacted within a universe that is indifferent yet autonomous—mysterious and stable, decaying and regenerative—a world of entropy and eternal renewal.

But time and space as existential or mechanical dimensions are further complicated by the psychological experience of them, and here Beckett stretches the paradoxes of human comprehensibility and adaptability even further. If, given the gratuitous events that require continuously adaptive stratagems, the will is continually self-renewing, the individual functions against an equally mysterious and autonomous force of the eternal unconscious, where time, space, and another sort of determinism operate in additionally mysterious configurations.

Thus portraying the multiple levels of psychological, existential, and mechanical time and space that are integral parts of his canvas, Beckett goes beyond the mere rejection of traditional narrative dramaturgy and character development to make space, time, the senses, and logic take on the dimensions of characters on stage. The forces that war with one another and determine the boundaries of human freedom are so complex and of such infinite power that he gives them a function once reserved for the Olympic deities in classical drama.

With the interplay of time and space so prominent in the play, it becomes very difficult to isolate the meaning and motivation of single words or lines because each demands an evaluation vis-à-vis all the others, and then a reevaluation within the multiple contexts of time and place in which each functions. The image of Chinese boxes within boxes is appropriate here, as Beckett's stage directions reinforce how, for example, a gesture performed in front of the tree or rock or an activity replayed multiple times may be both existentially unique and a variation of a single, constant emotional experience. Meaning *at that point* is dependent upon the spatial location in which it is enacted.

A single word may also reflect a different time and place in the speaker's life, depending upon which hat he is wearing or whether his pants are up or down. Meaning and motivation become as fluid and accretive as single words or gestures and function like isolated facets in a Cubist painting, in which the briefest sequence cuts across time and space, and the perceiver, with the power of associative or linear memory, juxtaposes the fragment against circular, vertical, or cosmic time. The part is thus integrated within the totality of the other facets and shifting planes of the design, like the circular or oval dimension of a teacup, which in its many-sidedness is impossible to represent on a flat canvas. Indeed, Beckett's manipulations of time and space recall a broad range of art, from the Impressionists to the Abstract and Geometrical Expressionists, in which vertical and horizontal time is simulated in order to convey the complexities of perception, logic, and final human incomprehensibility. *Godot*'s every word and gesture resounds in a void of silence, and the purity of Beckett's minimalist designs echoes with everything unsaid, the infinite polyphony and silence of the universe. The ultimate absurd paradox is that an indefinite possibility of meanings accrues to a world without definition.

THREE

The Dream as a Manifestation of Unconscious Language and Emotion: The Conglomerative Effect

QUERY: When we are dreaming and, as often happens, have a dim consciousness of the fact and try to wake, do we not say and do things which in waking life would be insane? May we not then sometimes define insanity as the inability to distinguish which is the waking and which the sleeping life? We often dream without the least suspicion of unreality. "Sleep hath its own world," and it is often as lifelike as the other.

Lewis Carroll, Diary, February 9, 1856

Dreams are the royal road to the unconscious.

Sigmund Freud

The power of *Waiting for Godot* derives from its exposure of the emotional life in counterpoint to the existential condition—Beckett's revelation of the unconscious feelings that accompany the quest for salvation in a world bereft of meaning. *Godot*'s much-repeated "'Let's go.' *(They do not move.)*" epitomizes not just the tension of individual action in a meaningless world; it also demonstrates the limits of will set against the constraining and deterministic forces of a controlling psyche. Condensing the tension between the human condition and human nature, the "Let's go . . ." refrain is a key to Beckett's new dramatic form, a measure of human freedom and constraint over both the inner and outer worlds, each of which is equally purposive, mysterious, and uncontrollable.

The following discussion concentrates on Freudian theory for two reasons. First, Beckett was well acquainted with and, I believe, highly influenced by Freudian thought. Second, Freud's descriptions of the intermingling of conscious and unconscious thought provide an uncanny new means with which to approach Beckett's work. Among his activities in the late twenties and thirties (see chapter 1), Beckett worked with the French Surrealists, discussed the workings of the unconscious with his friend and mentor James Joyce, and read Freud, whose works he owned, extensively.[1]

Beckett also gained firsthand knowledge of unconscious process from his own extensive dream analysis with Wilfred Bion, and he absorbed the rhythms of unconscious thought patterns from the patients at the London mental hospital where he worked. That he was fascinated with the "excavations of the deepest self" was apparent in his essay in "Exagmination Round His Factification," on Joyce's language as well as in his *Proust* monograph. Both revealed his interest in the artist's "nonlogical" thoughts "before they [had] been distorted into intelligibility [and] cause and effect," those moments of "descent" into the "explosive" and "unruly" parts of self.[2] Beckett is also said to have described his own preverbal recollections in the womb,[3] which Otto Rank called the subject matter of dreams.[4]

During this period, countless intellectuals and artists were debating and incorporating into their work the new Freudian theory; many of their ideas reappeared in Beckett's writing. One of Bergson's statements, for example, on the differences between the waking and dream state, anticipates the dot-circle image in Beckett's first novel, *Watt*. Bergson writes,

> I will tell you what you do when you are awake. You take me, the me of dreams, me the totality of your past, and you force me, by making me smaller and smaller, to fit into the little circle that you trace around your present action. That is what it is to be awake, . . . to live the normal psychical life. It is to battle. It is to will. As for the dream, . . . it is the state into which you naturally fall when you let yourself go, when you no longer have the power to concentrate yourself upon a single point, when you have ceased to will. What needs much more to be explained is the marvelous mechanism by which at any moment you will obtain instantly, and almost unconsciously, the concentration of all that you have within you upon one and the same point.[5]

Beckett's novels *Watt* and *Murphy* are set in part in mental institutions, the natural locale in which to reveal his characters' inner voices, as they "murmured," "sang," "stated," and "cried." In the plays, however, Beckett could circumvent difficulties of narration and point of view and give direct exposition of the unconscious life. He could manipulate dialogue in order to replicate the mind both horizontally and vertically, both in its conscious and unconscious thought functioning. Beckett's audiences would become entranced by the juxtaposition of logical and illogical dialogue and action—as an evocation of normal, waking experience, where conscious and unconscious thought intermingle, or as an evocation of a dreamscape, where rational elements exist alongside irrational elements, the necessary ingredients that give cohesion or narrative movement to the dream. (Freud called this mechanism "secondary revision," often the residual, logical elements from daytime experience that "shaped the content of dreams." He continually repeated that dreams contained thoughts that were "indistinguishable from our waking thoughts.")[6] Beckett gave artistic expression to many of Freud's revolutionary discoveries, particularly those in *The Interpretation of Dreams,* which explored how unconscious thoughts can most readily be accessed in the dream work, the pictorial manifestation of a conflicted wish.

Godot's dislocations of time and space as well as its unique mixtures of banal dialogue, poetic incantation, and concretizations or contradictions of thought and feeling—all set within a frame of highly mannered farce and slapstick—give the play the unmistakable quality of a waking dream. In replicating these universal states of mind, dreams, Beckett's highly original dramatic rhetoric—his poetic polyphonies of linguistic, spatial, and temporal design—convey a sense of fantastic but undeniable reality.

Freud asserted that unconscious and dream thoughts contain a unique grammar and language dominated by condensation, displacement, paradox, and distortions of time and space. His frequently quoted description of unconscious language is striking in its applicability to Beckett's work:

> Logical laws of thought . . . do not apply . . . and this is true above all to the law of contradiction. Contrary impulses exist side by side, without cancelling each other out or diminishing each other. There is nothing [here] that could be compared with negation; and we perceive [the] exception that space and time are necessary forms of our mental acts. . . . There is nothing that corresponds to the idea of time; there is no recognition of the passage of time, and—a thing that is most remarkable and awaits consideration in philosophical thought—no alteration in its mental processes is produced by the passage of time. Wishful impulses [and] impressions, too . . . are virtually immortal.

Freud's terminology, here and elsewhere, not only provides a viable idiom with which to approach *Godot*'s complex verbal designs, but it also offers a new means of addressing Beckett's stage design.[7] A focus on production, in understanding Beckett's choreography of conscious and unconscious thought, is as important as a focus on dialogue and action.[8] As we shall see, rhythmic patterns and body movement bear an uncanny resemblance to the complex visual arrangements in dreams. The direction in which characters move their arms or feet is as integral to meaning as dialogue, since bodily movement manifests unconscious thought as significantly as verbal arrangements. Each is a condensation, displacement, or substitution, and ultimately a composite image of every other one. Vertical or diagonal movements across the stage, like the play's objects—boots, pants, rocks, leaves, bones, hats, the tree, road, moon, belt, baggage, rope, stool, watch, and pipe—take on different meanings for each character in the variety of his changing moods, geographical location, and roles. It is as though Beckett were weaving into his existential landscape a map of the unconscious world, again, either as it functions simultaneously with rational thinking or is transformed into a dreamscape: the verbal and visual constructs of the feeling of helplessness that accompanies verbalized, logical yearnings for wholeness. Each object, word, and movement ultimately becomes an emblem of the psychological, not just the philosophical, reality of waiting.

To simplify the remainder of this chapter, I want to make a few distinctions between conscious and unconscious thought processes.[9] The language of consciousness or secondary process, the language of waking, conscious life, is familiar to everyone. Most simply stated, it is the language of Aristotelian logic, the mode of Barbara. It is goal-directed and takes mechanical time and space for granted. Vladimir asks Pozzo, "What do you do when you fall far from help?" to which Pozzo replies, "We wait til we can get up. Then we go on." Primary process is the language of the unconscious, dreams, and schizophrenia,[10] and it has its own rules of structure. As Freud's statement above makes clear, conventional logic (causation), space, and time are inapplicable. In response to Pozzo's "What time is it?" Estragon says, "That depends what time of year it is." Since the organizing principle of primary process thought, "paralogic," with its condensations, displacements, and plastic representations, is unfamiliar to most, these rhetorical principles will be fully discussed and illustrated in the next chapter.

THE CONGLOMERATIVE EFFECT

Freud uses the term *conglomeration* in the process of collecting the fragmentary components of the dream. This is a concept akin to the mental operation of "secondary revision," which gives final shape and form to the compressed dream image.[11] In following Freud's procedure, I shall speak of the conglomerative effect or conglomerate refrain in order to indicate what traditionally would be called the dominant theme of the play, always in the form of thesis and antithesis, affirmation and negation—appropriate to the conflicted wish generating the image. As a result, in *Godot,* many verbal and visual details, in their multiple, distinctive guises and distortions, will constitute the central experience of waiting, of " 'Let's go.' *(They do not move.)*"—the subject of Beckett's play, from the obvious recapitulation of activities in acts I and II to the most subtle units that comprise each part.

Approaching this design is difficult. If traditional language is an arbitrary, metaphoric translation or construct of felt and perceived experience, then unconscious or dream language is a translation or construct of yet another, even more obscure experience, of raw psychic energy. As Freud defined the dream phenomenon, "We approach [it] with analogies, [for it is] a chaos, a cauldron full of seething excitation."[12] If one asks whether the emotional life can be isolated without the rational component of consciousness, the answer is that it cannot. Consciousness never entirely disappears from the unconscious; it merely takes on new forms of expression. The challenge in understanding *Godot* lies in translating the "caged dynamic" (Beckett's description of the play)[13] of both psychological and existential experience through the interplay of two thought processes that juxtapose thesis, antithesis, and perpetually absent synthesis. The task, in a sense, is to translate motion into linear and synthesized commentary. Again, Cubist designs come to mind.

In each of its manifestations, the conglomerative refrain is appropriately inconclusive, or, in Lucky's repeated word, unfinished (understandably so, as a manifestation of the conflicting unconscious desire generating it and befitting the existential condition). *Unfinished* describes the relationship of each character to the universe, to nature, to his partner, and to himself, in terms of the complexities of mind function. *Inconclusive* similarly characterizes the structure of the play. That is, like Lucky's "unfinished" speech, a series of clauses that lack resolution, the play's two acts (each of which plays out Lucky's speech) lack a resolving third act. Each of the two acts, in turn, has an unsettling, precariously resolving tripartite construction: (1) Vladimir and Estragon "play" before Lucky and Pozzo arrive; (2) they are distracted by their "guests," after which (3) Godot fails to arrive, and they restore the equilibrium of their earlier interaction, but this is accomplished only after a discussion of suicide. Finally, Beckett introduces, within each of these divisions, numerous "unfinished" events, like Vladimir's song, an aborted yet repeated tale of a dog.

But as unfinished as these may be, it is "the shape that matters" (Beckett's phrase) in clarifying the conglomerative effect that underlies the whole.[14] I begin with an attempt to isolate the recurrent shape of the longer speeches, in which Beckett's figures articulate the isolation and helplessness that underscore so much of *Godot*. Lucky's monologue ("Given the existence. . .") is an obvious starting point, for, as chaotic as it appears, it is the play's most detailed expression of human achievement performed in the face of mortality and cosmic indifference.

Lucky's monologue, in three divisions, is a disjointed worldview of a onetime philosopher-poet: (1) The universe is ruled by an enigmatic, capricious deity: "Given the existence . . . of a personal God . . .

who from the heights of divine apathia divine athambia divine aphasia loves us dearly with some exceptions for reasons unknown"; (2) the human creature "wastes and pines" despite all the "strides" and "labors of men," intellectual, social, and physical; (3) only a stony, indifferent earth survives; all labors are "abandoned" and "left unfinished," in a landscape scattered with decayed bones—"the skull the skull"—the relics of human habitation.

Almost every word and activity in the play is an incremental repetition of this worldview. Each speaker comes to Lucky's wisdom and becomes a modern-day "Atlas," a spiritually and emotionally burdened innocent, bearing the world's best hopes on his shoulders. Lucky is a maddened Sisyphus whose heavy bags seem filled with the rubbish of intellectual endeavor and with the bone and sand that are a reminder of the end that awaits humanity. Yet Lucky continues and waits in his own fashion. On the day the tree blossoms, he becomes speechless. Like the other figures on stage, Lucky endures as he demonstrates the human incapacity to comprehend the entropic yet undiminishing energy of both human endeavor and natural event. Each character is an example, in word and appearance, of how any effort to order the world in thought or logic is a form of madness or folly. Wearing a thinking hat, like Lucky's, one is virtually incoherent; without it, mute. Yet one persists.

Even Pozzo, who dared measure, predict, and manipulate time, in the end accepts Lucky's wisdom. Pozzo has believed that he could control his life, but one day (words he repeats frequently) he realizes and concretely demonstrates the blindness of his ways. Having stretched human freedom to social and economic excess and possessed of the arrogance that he can control even the sunrise, the sightless Pozzo eventually reaches Lucky's conclusion: human accomplishment is futile in the face of an indifferent, if not malign, ruling force, which he addresses as the same undefined "they" who beat Estragon. Just as Pozzo's memorable speech—"One day we were born, one day we shall die, the same day, the same second"—is a dark echo of Ecclesiastes 3:3, "[There is] a time to be born, and a time to die," Pozzo follows a long line of literary archetypes who take good fortune for granted and learn too late the blindness of their ways. He is a modern-day Lear, on the road to nakedness and unaccommodation, to madness and truth. Lear's words to Edgar would ring true to Pozzo and Beckett's other characters: "Pull off my boots: harder, harder"; Lear continues, "We came crying hither: / Thou know'st, the first time that we smell the air / We wawl and cry" (IV.vi.180–82).

Yet Pozzo persists and in the end gains a redemptive innocence, not from an intervening God or fate but from the audience, which, like Vladimir and Estragon, come to pity him and understand how, as he says, life passes from day to nighttime in an instant. His speech is the most dramatic moment in the play's rising conclusion, and it parallels Lucky's speech at the climactic point of act I. It recaptures a brief, earlier image of Pozzo when, even at the height of his powers, he fought moments of desperation. To be Lucky's master has been overwhelming: "I'm going mad . . . *(he collapses, his head in his hands)* . . . I can't bear it . . . any longer." Despite this unusual display of vulnerability in act I, he quickly recovers his equanimity: "Gentlemen, I don't know what came over me. Forgive me. Forget all I said." Even so, he continues: "I have such need of encouragement." As repugnant as Pozzo's actions have been, he has taken on the task of providing his "knook" with direction, the very thing Vladimir and Estragon urgently seek. That Beckett intended for Pozzo to be portrayed as a needy character is clear in his direction that he "not be played as a superior figure (as he usually is)" because Pozzo "*plays* the *lord*—magnanimous, frightening—only because he is unsure of himself" (emphasis added).[15]

Pozzo has been educated by Lucky, the mad, childlike, onetime poet who knows that the end result of all human endeavor is excrement, in Lucky's words, "waste," "defecation," "caca" ("acacacacademy," the end product of study). But just as Lucky has taught Pozzo about time and human limitation, Pozzo's blindness and remarks on time propel Vladimir toward his own epiphany near the end of the play, and his words are another variation of the conglomerative effect. Vladimir's conclusion and some of his words are identical to Pozzo's:

POZZO: They give birth astride of a grave, the light gleams an instant, then it's night once more.
VLADIMIR: Astride of a grave and a difficult birth. Down in the hole, lingeringly, the gravedigger puts on the forceps.

Pozzo and Lucky have been created as inhabitants of a linear world, that is, with seeming direction and purpose (appropriate to Pozzo's illusion that he can control his life), and, unlike Vladimir and Estragon, their life activities take place both on- and offstage. In effect, Pozzo and Lucky function for Estragon and Vladimir, in their own fixed and circular world, like both ends of a binocular lens. While Pozzo and Lucky seem to have mastered their own games of survival—however ostensibly sadomasochistic: Pozzo holds the rope while promising to abandon Lucky; Lucky threatens his own freedom by refusing Pozzo's bones—they are magnified versions of Vladimir and Estragon in their mutual needs, resentments, and loneliness. They are reminders of their past (their earlier, more worldly life near the Eiffel Tower, Rhône River, and Macon country), but they are likewise prophetic of the decay that awaits them.

Before and after these revelatory speeches, Pozzo and Lucky function as catalysts that release Vladimir and Estragon's frustration and hostility, those "perilous zones of being," apparent but muted during their cordial games of camaraderie. Only after observing the debilitated Pozzo and Lucky do Vladimir and Estragon become more aggressive toward their guests, now hostage to their benevolence. After a brief show (or release) of hostility, Vladimir repeats Pozzo's words (Pozzo's "They give birth astride of a grave . . ." becomes

Vladimir's "Astride of a grave and a difficult birth . . ."), and with the synchronic and diachronic merging, the circular intersecting with the linear, each character demonstrates some understanding of himself and the world. Each regains a measure of primal innocence, assuming, as Beckett alludes to in the dialogue, a kinship with Adam, Cain, Abel, and a suffering but unredeemed Christ.

Notwithstanding this pattern of equilibrium, aggression, and insight, Beckett's vision would seem to be of a humanity more sinned against than sinning. In Vladimir's terms, humans are a species condemned to death, rather than to hell, gratuitously fallen through the mere act of birth, and they possess only the illusion of salvation; the reality of undeserved suffering and death is their only birthright. Beneath each character's purposive effort to seek salvation or direction is the haunting lament, "My God, my God, why hast Thou forsaken me?" Blindness, like Pozzo's, and silence, like Lucky's, are their only recompense: conglomerate images of the ultimate wasting and pining of body, mind, and spirit, the nonredemptive suffering to which all are condemned.

In discussing the conglomerative effect thus far, I have focused on the theme of oblivion rather than human accomplishment. It is this other aspect of the conflicted wish—again potentially realized in *either* "Let's go" *or* "They do not move"—that grants Beckett's figures their heroic, if not tragic, status. In the face of inevitable frustration, anxiety, and oblivion, Beckett's characters have choices: to capitulate, to endure the boredom of life, or, if the occasion arises, to perform acts of kindness. Stoicism and altruism may be unredemptive in terms of a responsive cosmic agency, but they offer moments of personal regeneration.

In act II, Vladimir steps outside of his circumscribed role—"Let us not waste our time in idle discourse"—and calls for both stoicism and generosity to others, demanding, specifically, that he and Estragon uplift the fallen Pozzo and Lucky. He then remarks on the uniqueness of the moment: "It is not every day that we are needed. . . . Let us make the most of it, before it is too late." Despite Vladimir's awareness of the human species' questionable moral worth (including his own; in his words, humanity is a "foul brood"), he affirms the imperative of going beyond one's meanest urges to altruistic action: "Come, let's get to work!" He asks "To be, or not to be" in his own terms: "What are we doing here?" and in the silence occasioned by his question, he rejects aggression toward both himself and others. At the same time, he reconfirms the only viable life alternative: that they wait and accept their act of waiting, along with whatever interrupts their games, *as* their life: "We are not saints, but we have kept our appointment." Implied is his understanding that since "the readiness is all," he must make the best of whatever fortune bestows in the act of passing the time. He is not unlike King Lear, who, when a father at last, tells his daughter Cordelia that in their imprisonment they will care for one another and "pray and sing and tell old tales, and laugh."

In waiting, Vladimir continues, echoing Lucky's references to the "labors of men," any game or routine invested with meaning, any man-made ritual, will deaden the pain and boredom while sustaining reason, Vladimir's most valued endowment: "All I know," he says, "is that the hours are long . . . and constrain us to beguile them with proceedings . . . which may at first sight seem reasonable." The danger lies in the possibility that calculated procedures may degenerate into thoughtless habit or routine, which would then permit reason to stray to the inevitable conclusion that all proceedings are, in their very enactment, meaningless, as is demonstrated by the reality of human ignorance, Beckett's folly or madness.

But "has [reason] not long been straying in the night. . . ?," Vladimir rhetorically asks his more instinctive partner, who replies with the ultimate truth of *Godot:* "We were all born mad. Some remain so," a sensibility he has expressed through much of the play. Here again is the statement that the mere act of birth defines our Fall. The Manichean gnosticism permeating the conglomerative effect has now been uttered by Estragon, Vladimir, Lucky, and Pozzo.

In a subsequent speech, "Astride of the grave . . .", Vladimir echoes Pozzo's and Lucky's comments. A beautifully sculpted passage, Vladimir's words flow in concentric circles that spin off one another and reflect the circular inquisitions he has pursued during a lifetime of waiting and wondering. His impulses toward action and inaction, toward acceptance and despair, alternate. He begins by asking, "Was I sleeping while the others suffered?" which recalls "The tears of the world are a constant quantity," Beckett's exquisite statement about the alternation of joy and suffering in the human experience. As he looks at his friend, Estragon, he is overwhelmed by hopelessness, unsure of the purposefulness of their activities, unsure of reality itself. This is the dark night of his soul ("I can't go on!"), yet he repudiates capitulation: "What have I said?"

In this, Vladimir's recognition speech, he reviews his life. In a moment of bleak pessimism, he realizes that not only may his lifelong philosophical questions remain unanswered, but he may also lack verification that his ordinary daily activities have meaning or, for that matter, have even occurred: "To-morrow when I wake, or think I do, what shall I say of to-day? That . . . I waited for Godot? . . . Probably." And of this, he adds, "What truth will there be?"

Vladimir looks at Estragon and ponders the futility of his inquiries. Estragon is dozing, and Vladimir, who has revered reason as a means of reaching truth, says of him: "He'll know nothing," unaware that perhaps, as Democritus thought, nothing ("naught") is "more real than nothing"—in Beckett's world, truth lies beyond reason. Indeed, Estragon may be the wiser one in understanding that reality is entirely irrational, an intellectual void, a nightmare or just a dream.[16] Even Vladimir wonders several times in this passage if he is sleeping as he speaks: "Am I sleeping now?" he asks, and "To-morrow when I wake or think I do. . ." After the gravedigger speech, however, he rebounds, and in an affirmative voice reconfirms the only area of human activity that is meaningful, even if it is metaphysically unverifiable and forgotten the next day. One can care for another ("He is sleeping . . . let him sleep on"). One can overcome cosmic and personal loneliness by listening to the childlike cries of men lamenting the blows they received and offering them pacifiers like carrots, by momentarily altering the balance of tears and laughter that mark the human experience.

Turning his rational inquisitions to the quintessential question, he wonders if, in the end, there is purpose in any of his activities. Perhaps another person—or Godot—looks upon him as he looks upon Estragon and concludes that he knows nothing: "At me too someone is looking, of me too, someone is saying He is sleeping, he knows nothing, let him sleep on."[17] In the end, Vladimir does not act upon his statement "I can't go on." Instead, he concludes "What have I said?" He reconsiders his assertion "We have time to grow old," even though "the air is full of our cries," and affirms not only their waiting but the virtue of how they wait, with "habit . . . [the] great deadener"—with their self-made games and rituals, the only anesthetic to the pain of being.

And so the game resumes, with Vladimir's brooding, Beckett's description of him at the start of the play. He and his partner are ready to greet Godot's messenger, and their repeated "Let's go" and "They do not move" recapitulates the conglomerative effect: their return to wavering between hope deferred (Augustine) and hope maintained (Matthew). The refrain again underscores the conflict between conscious and unconscious motivation, the paralysis inevitable from an inconclusive knowledge of the self and universe—and once more, like Lucky's speech with its absence of a final independent clause, their defining, if inconclusive waiting. I shall return to these speeches at the end of the book.

The conglomerative effect recurs throughout the play. For example, Vladimir says, "We wait. We are bored. . . . A diversion comes along and what do we do? We let it go to waste. Come let's go to work! In an instant all will vanish and we'll be alone again, in the midst of nothingness." Many lines focus on human oblivion: "To each man his little cross until he is forgotten"; "There's no protesting it. We are born to death." That one is born to no purpose is repeated in the many uses of *nothing*: not just the initial "Nothing to be done" and the "nothingness" of the first citation above, but also "What's wrong with you?" and the response, "Nothing" and "[We've] been blathering about nothing. That's been going on for half a century" and, perhaps the most devastating observation of all, the messenger's remark that Mr. Godot "does nothing."

In expressing the conglomerative effect through several characters and in very similar terms, Beckett seems to be merging his characters into a single, generic voice, demonstrating, as Freud observed, that unconscious thought can manifest itself in the serialization of the single self, in any number of seemingly separate figures.[18] That is why, at any given moment, Vladimir and Estragon may function as individual characters or as two halves of a single whole, just as each of the four, six, seven, or even eight characters of the play, including the absent Mr. Godot(s), may function independently or as a mirror of each other or as merging elements of a single whole. As we shall see, Beckett's figures merge into a composite Cain-Abel figure, the Old Testament's first innocent victims in a gratuitously capricious, unfathomable universe.

Even at the beginning, the simplest matters of identity are obfuscated. In the text, the characters are designated as Vladimir and Estragon both in the stage directions as well as before their dialogue. On stage, however, they address or speak of each other as Didi and Gogo. The messenger mistakes Vladimir for Mr. Albert (Camus?), and Pozzo at first appearance is mistaken for Godot, Bozzo, and perhaps someone from a family named Gozzo; Pozzo twice confuses Godot with Godet and Godin. The identity of the messenger boys, who have the same defective memory as Estragon, Pozzo, and Lucky's deity, is also unclear, just as it is unclear if Mr. Godot has a black or white beard.[19] At various moments, all the characters, either directly or by implication, call themselves Cain or Abel, Adam or Christ. Ultimately, each figure is tied to another and operates in a world of complex and frequently paradoxical literary, biblical, and historical referents. To modify Pozzo's remark, not only might each have been in the other's shoes, a key emblem in the play, but in fact each is.

FOUR

The Conglomerative Voice: Cain and Abel

VLADIMIR: I tell you his name is Pozzo.

ESTRAGON: We'll soon see. . . . Abel! Abel! . . . Perhaps the other is called Cain. Cain! Cain! . . . He's all humanity.

. . . .

VLADIMIR: You work for Mr. Godot?

BOY: Yes Sir. . . . I mind the goats, Sir.

VLADIMIR: Is he good to you?

BOY: Yes Sir. . . .

VLADIMIR: He doesn't beat you?

BOY: No Sir, not me.

VLADIMIR: Whom does he beat?

BOY: He beats my brother. . . . He minds the sheep, Sir.

VLADIMIR: And why doesn't he beat you?

BOY: I don't know, Sir.

VLADIMIR: He must be fond of you.

BOY: I don't know, Sir.
Silence.

> And the Lord had respect unto Abel and to his offering.
> But unto Cain and to his offering he had not respect.
>
> *Genesis 4:4–5*[1]

If the conglomerative effect is expressed by each character, Beckett creates, as in a dream, serialized components of what might be called a single, conglomerative voice. This voice retells, in a timeless landscape, the biblical story of Cain and Abel, the primal archetypes of innocence and brutality. The world of *Godot* is as mysterious in design as that of Genesis 4; both are set within a universe in which grace and punishment are gratuitously imposed.

Primordial examples of innocent selfhood and corrupted brotherhood, Cain and Abel are the first children on earth and, as the Bible presents them, are literally "all humanity." Born after the Fall, they have only each other as witness to their existence, and as they complement one another—Cain, a tiller of the earth; Abel, a shepherd and wanderer—they are subject to a God who, in a sense, beats one child and rewards the other. The brothers' loyalty to each other and to God is tested before the Old Testament's covenantal partnership between God and Abraham and before the New Testament's revelation of a Christ who will redeem the sins of humanity. Like Vladimir and Estragon, Cain and Abel are called upon to define themselves as brotherly in a universe bereft of definition.

The biblical lesson, as Beckett transcribes it, is that although we should be our brother's keeper, we are ruled, as Lucky puts it, by a divinity who loves us "dearly with some exceptions for reasons unknown." Now, as then, human goodness and suffering are imposed by capricious external and internal forces. The characters in Genesis and *Godot* face the same fate: punishment is exacted for what seem to be the best of intentions, and the sufferers are condemned to the charnel-house with, in Lucky's terms, an unfinished explanation of their verdict.

Beckett's choice of Cain and Abel as prototypes of the conglomerative voice is particularly interesting if one considers Cain and possibly his twin or double, Abel, as the first tragic figures in biblical literature.[2] Thrust into a universe that lacks a moral order—Where are their parents? What divine laws have been declared for these, the first post-Edenic children?—Cain is gratuitously motivated toward goodness. He offers the first gift in human history to God but is rejected, rebuked, provoked, and finally condemned by the very God he seeks to please. In the absence of Adam and Eve, the Divine Father might have comforted, if not intervened, in the sequences that drive Cain to murder. Instead, He exacerbates Cain's growing despair. After a series of deceptive questions, He also tests him: Choose goodness, He says, which will please Me; otherwise, overcome sin, which is at your door. After this, the murder occurs, and God poisons any portion of earth that Cain would cultivate and condemns this tiller of the soil to a life of wandering and godlessness.

Unlike Ixion, whom Zeus exonerates for committing the first murder (Ixion is also ignorant of the uniqueness of his violence—that is, that it will result in death), and unlike Oedipus, who chooses social and spiritual exile, Cain would embrace death rather than accept exile from home, work, and, most insufferably, from God, a triple exile implied in Beckett's landscape. To him, such a fate is intolerable: "My punishment is greater than I can bear. Thou has driven me out from the face of the earth, and from Thy face shall I be hid, and I shall be a fugitive and wanderer on the earth." God then banishes Cain to perpetual wandering, isolation, and loneliness. In order to prevent his death by murder, God brands him. Some argue that Cain's exile is a test and pathway toward redemption, but the text is ambiguous on this matter.[3] Unlike Job, who eventually gains a new family and fortune and who enjoys a long, fulfilled life, Cain settles in the land of Nod (or "restlessness," Genesis 4:16), where he knows no peace and is murdered by his brutal and arrogant blood brother Lamech (Genesis 4:23–24).

To the modern reader, the Bible's silence regarding its principal characters, Cain, Abel, and perhaps the central figure, God, is troubling. But as biblical commentators have remarked, God's relationship to His children alters radically after the Fall. In Eden, God walked and talked amid creation. Now, He removes himself from intimacy with His children. By Genesis 4, Adam and Eve's first offspring are thrust into a universe whose external rules or Law are as mysterious, arbitrary, and potentially destructive as the forces that motivate their choices and instinctive behavior. Nevertheless, consensus regarding the chapter's meaning has most frequently embraced the moral imperative that, regardless of life's injustices, we *are* our brother's keeper.

The text, however, suggests that moral goodness, even at the most elementary level, must be learned. In this light, Cain's question, "Am I my brother's keeper?" is not rhetorical. Cain is asking God *if* he is responsible for his brother; one cannot assume that Cain would have instinctively demonstrated fraternal responsibility: the tale takes place, after all, after the Fall. And even if one accepted that the question was rhetorical, one would be forced to ask why Abel was not Cain's keeper when he suffered God's rejection. Shouldn't Abel, who copied and bettered his brother's gift giving and who witnessed Cain's growing despair, have been sensitive to his brother's discountenance by God? Although Adam and Eve did not understand the meaning of death (nor would Cain, like Ixion, until after the murder), God at least ordained their prohibition, after which they chose to rebel. Evil, in other words, was a part of their world design; in Genesis 3, the serpent was created before God's interdiction, and Adam and Eve, despite their ignorance of their subsequent punishment, were given divine warning. But for Cain and Abel, no prohibition or law regarding familial or social relationship was pronounced, even though punishment was imposed.

The early chapters of Genesis establish a world of human evil from Eden until the appearance of Noah and his family. Not until Abraham is born does God design the covenantal relationship between humankind and Himself, the universal moral bond connecting Him to all who are created in His image. It is not until Exodus that the Ten Commandments are carved for humankind. Only then are a universal law and its concomitant moral anchorage established, from which one may derive a sense of limitation and purpose—the I-Thou relationship through which one may perhaps help God in moving the universe toward ultimate perfection and through which one may gain the means to personal salvation. Before the covenant and the commandments, violence, rebellion, and evil would seem to be the natural propensity in human affairs.

To a religious existentialist like Elie Wiesel, Cain's deed is a frustrated act against divine injustice, a defiant but "loving gesture" against the human condition of passivity, as well as a response to his parent's ejection from paradise. Cain's violence, Wiesel continues, is also intended as his escape from fate. It is intended as an act of suicide, for Cain could not have known that murder and suicide are alternate expressions of the same instinct.[4]

The Cain and Abel story is interesting alongside *Godot* for many reasons. The story's locale is everywhere; it is undefined except for a field and rock. The time is after creation, when evil and guilt have entered the world. Like Vladimir and Estragon, God's children are condemned to live without understanding the nature of sin and eventual suffering. The brothers also complement each other. Cain, a farmer by trade, is a doer: he must attend to his fruits and plough the earth. Abel, a shepherd, wanders the roadways and, by biblical tradition, when watching his sheep graze, is a dreamer, perhaps a poet. Some readers say that he marvels "at the rustling of leaves," a particularly striking image, since it reappears in *Godot*.[5]

Written in a few terse sentences, Genesis 4 has a density that is rare in the Bible and is filled with ironies, paradoxes, puns, number play, and wordplay.[6] When Eve announces the birth of Cain she says, "I have gotten a man from the Lord"; in many translations "acquired" or "created" is substituted for "gotten": "I have acquired a child with the help of the Lord,"[7] the beginning of a play on the word *acquisition,* which is the meaning of Cain's name.[8] The brothers' names have similar meanings and foreshadow their fate. Cain means not only "acquire", but also "full-blown" and "smith" or "forge," "create," and "fashion," as well as its opposite "disappear" and "reed" or "stalk." The name Cain suggests the need and futility of acquisition and creativity; all human acts indicate the fragility and vanity of human accomplishment, in Lucky's terms. Abel's name is less complicated but identical in meaning to Cain's. It means "puff," "nothingness," or "breath": "Man is like a breath, his days, a passing shadow" (Psalms 144:4). Both names suggest, as Lucky's speech details, the futility of human achievement, the futility of life itself. The brothers' names also point to their vocations. Cain, derived from the Hebrew stem *k-y-k,* creates or fashions life out of the earth; Abel, from the Hebrew stem *n-v-l,* also means "herdsman." If, like his father, Cain cultivates the land, Abel pursues a complementary profession that was unnecessary in paradise but now is essential for survival: he supplies hides and wool for clothing. Their offerings reflect their differing roles. That the brothers are two halves of a whole, the rural and the urban man, the corrupt city and the innocent pastoral state, has been noted by many scholars.[9] This is perhaps a distinction to be made between Vladimir/Estragon and Lucky/Pozzo. Unlike the shepherd Abel, who precedes the tradition of the nomadic or shepherding patriarchs Moses and David, Cain is an acquirer, a peasant, a settler. By definition in Sumerian literature as well as in the Bible, settlers were slaves to possessions and were prone to corruption and idolatry; they were the builders of the sinister, degenerate cities.[10]

The tale suggests that brothers have no choice as to whether or not they will be each other's victim or victimizer.[11] Because of inscrutable forces, in this instance God or their own innate violence, they live with the possibility of being each other's protector or destroyer or both. Given the arbitrariness of God's actions in Genesis 4, the Cain–Abel myth plays out God's declaration in Exodus 33:19: "I will be gracious to whom I will be gracious and will shew mercy on whom I will shew mercy." Godot was similarly kind to one of the messengers and cruel to the other. One of the thieves was saved, one condemned.

God's capriciousness is apparent throughout, and the reader is particularly distressed by His preference of one child over the other. The Father demonstrates an inexplicable partiality toward Abel's offering of the "firstlings of his flock," after rejecting Cain's "fruit of the ground." From an anthropological-historical point of view, it is possible to argue that Abel's gift is more appropriate than Cain's in that the fattened animal would be used in ceremonial sacrifice. One might also argue that Cain's killing of Abel is an instance of precovenantal human sacrifice (recall Abraham and Isaac) in order to reinvigorate the land—an act instigated by Abel's gift and served by his blood. Ritual sacrifice would fertilize the soil with the blood of renewal.

As though the Omniscient could not understand Cain's initial humiliation, He goads his crestfallen son and asks him why he is distressed and ashamed: "Why art thou wroth? And why is thou countenance fallen?" And without waiting for a response, He proceeds to lecture Cain on temptation: Good deeds, He says, will uplift you and please Me; otherwise, you will be motivated by evil urges, which you can subsequently master: "If thou doest well, shall thou not be accepted? and if thou doest not well, sin lieth at the door. And unto thee shall be his desire, and thou shalt rule over him." The New English Bible eliminates Cain's capability to conquer temptation: "If you do well, you hold your head up; if not, sin is a demon crouching at the door; it will master you, and you will be mastered by it." The problem with both readings is that Cain has just done well by making an offering, yet he has not received God's pleasure.

Rather than encourage Cain to open his heart and partake in a dialogue that might clarify his confusion and shame—that is, rather than establish a relationship with His son that might obviate the subsequent violence—God delivers this sermon. But its message is abstract and ambiguous. Announcing that sin lies at Cain's door and that Cain can rule over "him,"[12] God may be planting the idea of Cain's subsequent action against his brother. On the other hand, He may be testing his faith, demanding that the innocent and generous Cain forgive his competitive favored brother. Following God's advice, Cain and Abel meet in the field, the postlapsarian garden. Cain has taken God's words as a directive, as a way of affirming his identity by action. However, like Ixion, he is unaware of the concrete implications of that action. God has used the words *sin* and *urge,* whatever they may mean.[13]

Possibly behind God's sermon is His assumption, as St. Augustine later writes, that after the Fall, sinful humanity *must be taught morality.* That is, even when one acts righteously (one makes offerings), evil lingers in the heart. If this is the case, God has read Cain's darkest instincts and judged that his offering was made from impure motives.[14] Yet modernist questions persist: Is one responsible for unconscious motivations as well as for the innate fallen state? Is one responsible for human nature and the human condition?

The gratuitousness of God's unkindness continues, and additional parallels with Beckett's play are apparent. The Cain–Abel story is the first example of dialogue in the Bible, and yet it illustrates how language avoids or obscures communication. Indeed, the very answer Cain gives to God's "Where is your brother?"—"Am I my brother's keeper?"—is troubling in its very formulation. Not only does it function in a sequence in which God is speaking disingenuously, for surely God knows where Abel is, but in responding to the question of fraternal responsibility, Cain is asked to account to an authoritative voice that refuses to be authoritative. Furthermore, in reply to Cain's question "Am I my brother's keeper?" God is silent and proceeds to inform Cain of His knowledge of the murder: "What hast thou done? The voice of thy brother's blood crieth out unto me from the ground."

If one assumes that God's question "Where is your brother?" is preparatory to Cain's confession, then one is prompted to ask if God Himself should not be responsive to Cain's crisis. Should He not be His children's keeper? Where, after all, was God when this first of human murders took place? Again, no answer is implied, and God's question "What hast thou done?," like his earlier response to Cain's first despair ("Why art thou distressed?"), reminds one of His interrogations after Adam and Eve's Fall in 3:9: "And the Lord called unto Adam and said unto him, Where art thou?" And in 3:11, He asks, "Hast thou eaten of the tree, whereof I commanded thee that thou shouldst not eat?" Again, although Adam and Eve's act occurred in the context of an articulated law, Cain is called upon to account to a moral standard that has never been revealed. Indeed, some commentators read God's "The voice of thy brother's blood crieth out unto me from the ground" to mean "Your brother's blood cries out *against* me."[15]

The most important section of the text takes the form of silence—not unlike the silences that fill *Godot*—when the brothers meet in the field and speak. One can only surmise that their interchange might clarify Cain's subsequent violence, as it might reveal any number of other important facts, such as whether or not Abel understood his brother's despair and whether or not Abel was aggressive or passive in their confrontation. What is clear, however, is that Cain initiates the meeting: "And Cain talked with his brother." Aramaic Targums, like Greek, Syriac, and Latin versions, add another of Cain's statements to the text: "Let us go into the field." The pivotal omission centers on the nature of their encounter. The Bible passes over it in silence: "*And it came to pass,* when they were in the field, that Cain rose up against Abel his brother, and slew him" (emphasis added). In some editions, ellipses replace the uninformative "And it came to pass": "Cain said to his brother Abel . . . and when they were in the field, Cain set upon his brother Abel and killed him."[16] It is here that the Omniscient, following His "What hast thou done?" condemns Cain: "And now thou are accursed from the earth. . . . When thou tillest the ground it shall not henceforth yield unto thee her strength. A fugitive and a vagabond shalt thou be in the Earth." God has polluted the earth Cain tills, and, not unlike his father, Adam, whose name means "earth," Cain is to be a wanderer to every corner of the world.

Final questions regarding the quality of God's presence in the immediate post-Edenic world, questions not dissimilar to those posed by the modern existentialist, are troubling. In the absence of a guiding law, what are one's responsibilities? If uncertainty is the only given, may not any deed committed from will, passion, or even religious faith be ultimately judged, as Camus phrases it, in terms of one's irreparable innocence? May not Cain's murderous act, like Mersault's in *The Stranger,* have been incited by inscrutable external forces, like the blinding sun? In the earliest world of Genesis, as in *Godot,* may not evil thus result from the moral indeterminacy of an incomprehensible universe or from an inexplicable or arbitrary expression of will or instinct? And if it is these that propel one out of innocence or pure ignorance toward the unthinkable, then what is the meaning of sin and guilt, which depend on moral intention in the context of an absolute and knowable moral system, as opposed to crime and punishment, which depend on social definitions that may be relative, arbitrary, and pragmatic?

The brothers Cain and Abel are not unlike *Godot*'s people, who inhabit a world marked only by the historical reminiscence of Eden (the tree) and the rock that will forevermore symbolize and potentiate brotherly murder. The same gloom hangs over Beckett's universe as over that of Cain and Abel. Here, in the first instance of death and personal isolation, is the archetypal example of harmony and discord between brothers, one the tiller of the soil, the other the shepherd, two halves of a whole; the younger brother, like the older, become gift giver; the older, like the younger, become nomad; both passionate and indifferent to the plight of the other; both chosen; both suffering; each the prototype of all humanity. Lucky's monologue, with its various motifs about human endeavor and an arbitrary deity and its climactic unfinished comprehension of the universe, would seem entirely applicable to the spiritual impulse of Genesis 4. If this seems a bleak vision, it is mitigated by Beckett's emphasis on his characters' efforts to be their brother's keeper and perhaps, at times, to act as if "all humanity" were brothers.

FIVE

The Language of Dreams: The Anatomy of the Conglomerative Effect

"Play" [is the] natural activity of all living things (human animal), and its goal is beyond "self-preservation"; it is a way of removing the "burden" of human existence as it "deepens" our connection with ourselves. If the dream functions for the same purpose—as relief and continuity, one might suggest that *the dream* is all we have in our desperation; it is the modern equivalent of religion—a new (another) form of play, a form of relief without transcendence, without mysticism, our only would-be, not greatly successful, escape from pain.

Hans-Georg Gadamer

Dream thoughts . . . cannot . . . have any definite endings; they are bound to branch out in every direction into the intricate network of our world of thought.

Sigmund Freud

We have discussed dreams as absurd, but examples have taught us how sensible a dream can be even when it appears to be absurd.

Sigmund Freud

Having considered secondary revision and the conglomerative meaning of *Godot,* I can turn to the bizarre, illogical fragments and dialogue exchanges that compose a major part of the play. The dense, cryptic, contradictory nature of this material is accomplished by specific rhetorical devices akin to those described in *The Interpretation of Dreams.* The following includes examples of displacement, condensation, plastic pictorialization, and multiple manifestations of paralogic, all of which reject causation and temporal linearity. If, to Freud, intrapsychic mechanisms allow the individual disguised outlets (dreams) in which to express repressed (ego-censored) feelings, for Beckett they become unique poetic techniques with which to elaborate the conglomerate *emotional* experience—in *Godot,* the feeling of precarious survival in the incohesive worlds of self and the universe.

Freud described the dreamer as a poet but hastened to add that the final dream scenario would always remain unedited, a drama derived from an entirely personal vocabulary, and that final interpretation would be inconclusive. In addition, given the transformational energy propelling dreams, one could always anticipate a sense of excitement from the dream and an evocation of infinite meaning only rarely equaled in the theater.[1] Dreams are, after all, continuously innovative and improvisational, and since they are the creation of the dreamer they are never boring. Finally, these translations of psychic energy always generate wonder (Freud's word) from their unique construction upon vertical and horizontal spatial and temporal axes that reflect the continuously evolving and metamorphosing energy beneath dream transformations, as well as those elements of rational thought against which unconscious revelations continuously vibrate. All the same, to Freud, underlying, alinear patterns might allow one to decipher partial meanings, in addition to the conglomerative effect. In fact, one can be quite specific in outlining how the recurrence of certain patterns described by Freudian analysts as typical of dream or unconscious thought[2] provides what they call the grammar of *Godot.*

One might begin at any point in the play and trace transformational patterns via a variety of avenues: the unique rhythms of syntax and asymmetries of word association, the acoustical properties of words and their visual-verbal resemblances (homonyms), connotations acquired through alliteration, consonance and rhyming possibilities, the reversal of parts of speech, as well as metonymy, synecdoche, synesthesia, puns, personification, and oxymoron. For example, in *Godot* causal relations are obliterated, inverted, or set into contradiction. Estragon says, "Don't touch me! Don't question me! Don't speak to me! Stay with me!" Objects and events transform into one another: chicken bones become fish bones; night instantly transforms into day. The use of alternatives like either-or is similarly abandoned, with the result that both elements of disjunction are placed in a single context; in other words, either-or becomes both-and. As Beckett once said of him, Pozzo might be (a) Godot: he provides direction to Lucky and is mistaken for Godot when he appears.[3] Pozzo and Lucky, in addition, are at one and the same time master and slave to each other; Didi and Gogo's role reversals, discussed below, permit each to appear as the dependent, wise, or controlling figure.

The word *if,* which in logical thinking indicates wish or the conditional, is represented by simultaneity. In fact, the traditional logic implied in the use of conjunctions is entirely revised in unconscious thought process: *and, or, but, because, just as,* and *though* as well as *if* and *either-or* are indicated by simultaneity.[4] The need for a Godot is transformed into the belief that a meeting with him is imminent. All relations of similarity, correspondence, and contiguity are unified. Disjunctures of ordinary logic, time, and space, along with the absence of the conditional tense, result in the equation of the fantastic with the realistic. To Vladimir and Estragon, God is a businessman, consulting his family, friends, and bank accounts. It follows that when Pozzo appears before Vladimir and Estragon and is served his private communion of food and wine, he is mistaken for Godot. He presents himself as a successful entrepreneur who enjoys being treated, as he puts it, with "fear and trembling."

If the chain of these concretizations seems unending, so is the network of characters created from the aural and visual similarity of words (G*odot*/P*ozzo*/G*ogo;* Luck*y*/Did*i;* f*oot*/b*oot*); and from their bisyllabic (Didi/Gogo/Pozzo/Lucky) and trisyllabic pairings (Estragon/Vladimir), as well as pairings based on identical multiples from the alphabet: Estragon and Vladimir, consisting of eight letters; Pozzo/Lucky, five; Didi/Gogo, four; even more subtle is the construction of *D*idi's and *G*ogo's names after those of the two hanged thieves, *D*ysmas and *G*estas. (Beckett's pair frequently ponder the mystery of salvation and damnation.)

Dream images and characters, like unconscious thought, are also formulated upon the literal, foreign, and etymological roots of words. Didi, from *dire,* to speak, is the partner who contemplates and prefers that Lucky "think"; Gogo (to go), Didi's opposite, is more physical and sensual, and he would have Lucky "dance." Each, regardless of his role or role reversal, concretely represents some dimension or playing out of the conglomerative effect. If Pozzo, in Italian, means "well" or "hole," his name concretizes the pun and paradox of whole and hole, completeness and emptiness, another manifestation of the circular and paradoxically imperative but useless waiting in the play. The condensations of *Lucky* are similarly rich, with Lucky (1) apparently lucky in having his Godot in Pozzo, (2) illustrating the ambiguity and gratuitousness of luck, as Pozzo puts it, "I might just as well have been in his shoes and he mine. If chance had willed otherwise," (3) representing a modern-day Luke, patron saint of artists who wrote of the two thieves and also said, as Beckett ultimately implies, "The Kingdom of God(ot) is within you" (17:21). Luke is also iconographically associated with the calf, which is gastronomically associated with tarragon (in French, *estragon*). (4) Lucky is "raised" by Estragon and Vladimir in act I and is related to yet another biblical figure, *L*azarus. The list is endless—for another example, as a mad dancer, Lucky suggests Joyce's daughter, Lucia, also mad and a dancer.

Dream concretizations extend to the imprecise use of words and temporal dislocations: "Once in a way [not "while"]" and "Get up till I embrace you" (act I) and "Come here till I embrace you [not "so that I can"]" (act II)—and their simultaneously oppositional meanings. Lucky dances "The Net," which, like the rock (Peter's church / Cain's weapon in slaying Abel) and tree (the Garden of Eden / site of the Crucifixion), elicits multiple associations with emptiness and redemption (for example, captivity and rescue). These condensations enrich the sparse dialogue and setting with multiple levels of meaning.

A word may be repeated or used simultaneously as different parts of speech, once again reinforcing the conglomerative effect. When the four major characters fall, Beckett uses *fall* as both a noun and verb, and the figures fall down upon one another in the shape of a cross; at one time, the four form a double cruciform. The same holds true of their lifting up or raising of Pozzo and Lucky. As Beckett directed, when Lucky is uplifted, he is to stand between Vladimir and Estragon with outstretched arms, in another configuration of the cross.

Waiting, Vladimir and Estragon's paradoxical life activity, is repeated not just in the "Let's go. *(They do not move.)*" refrain but in subtle repetitions of the word *again,* generating both a sense of stasis and movement: *"Estragon gives up, exhausted, rests, tries again"* and Vladimir's "There you are again . . . There we are again . . . There I am again." Waiting, like the phrase "Nothing to be done," is concretely played out in many activities and verbal interchanges, such as in Vladimir and Estragon's waiting for Lucky to dance and for night to fall and in their repeated statements "Nothing happens," "Nobody comes, nobody goes, it's awful," and "What do we do now?" Beckett listed 109 instances of waiting in one Production Notebook, each an intended variation of the larger waiting for Godot.[5]

Vladimir's song at the beginning of act II generates its own sense of infinite regression or waiting—for a denouement. Repeating, without conclusion, the tale of a dog beaten to death by a cook, after which several dogs bury the dead, after which the dog is beaten to death, after which several dogs bury the dead . . . is another example of oblivion and gratuitous benevolence, another example of the conglomerative effect: a tale waiting for a conclusion. It is also a fitting introduction to a second act that repeats and elaborates upon this subject.

To return to the brief distinctions made in chapter 3 between dream or unconscious thought (primary process) and rational thought (secondary process), I want to explain the paralogic of primary process, which has its own unique rules of structure. In addition to being personalized, rather than goal directed, and often perceived as gibberish or nonsense, it is typified by non sequiturs, for it is not bound by the everyday usage of time and space. In addition, whereas in logical, secondary process, the subject of a minor premise is always included in the major one (for example, in All men are mortal. Socrates is a man . . . , "Socrates" is part of "all men"), in primary process paralogic, the subject of the minor premise is *never* included in the subject of the major one. For example, in Certain Indians are swift. Stags are swift, and so on, one would not rationally conclude that all stags are Indians. But in paralogic, objects may be equated on the basis of a single property, here, the common swiftness of stags and certain Indians.[6] In *Godot,* when Pozzo announces, "I am blind," Estragon paralogically connects blindness with Tiresias and then says of Pozzo, "Perhaps he can see into the future," as though all blind men were prophets; using the same kind of paralogic, Lucky says he is a poet because he wears rags. A more elaborate illustration and example of condensation is Vladimir's reply to Estragon's suggestion that they hang themselves. "Hmmm," he begins. "It'd [suicide] give us an erection." While it may be true that hanging causes this physiological reaction, Vladimir's subsequent remarks reinforce the entirely paralogical nature of his thoughts:

"With all that follows. Where it falls mandrakes grow. That's why they shriek when you pull them up. Did you not know that?" Mandrakes may have physical similarities with the human body, and shrieking and dying may, at least poetically, be associated with both the sexual act and the sound of the plant when it is uprooted, but Vladimir and Estragon are not plants, and the main issue under discussion is not sexual. Vladimir is unable or unwilling to rationally consider their suicide. The closest he gets to it, pursuing his paralogical thought further, is in his association of death, or the body's hanging, and the Fall. He says, "Where it falls mandrakes grow", but his "it" would seem to refer to his erection. To both Vladimir and Estragon, hanging is associated with the Fall, the result of the (original) sin of simply being born. Vladimir paralogically equates the visual similarity of an erection with hanging, along with his other associations of death, shrieking, and sexual response.

An even more intricate example of paralogic and condensation that highlights the complexities and contradictions of the conglomerative effect occurs in Vladimir's "Hope deferred maketh the something sick," a rewording of Proverbs 13:12, "Hope deferred maketh the heart sick: but when the desire cometh, it is a tree of life." Vladimir takes the first half of the statement concretely and concludes that postponing hope, that is, waiting for Godot, makes, so to speak, a vague "something" ill. The proverb rests on a belief in the future ("but when"): if one defers hope, one's heart aches, but when one regains faith (the "desire" to hope), one is reinvigorated or resurrected. Vladimir's collapsing of the conditional "but when" into a flat, declarative statement, "Hope maketh the something sick," militates against the option of change. Time or chronology, specifically, future redemption ("but when"), has been deleted.

"The something sick" restates the conglomerative effect that humankind "wastes and pines": Vladimir's pained loins, Estragon's feet, Pozzo's heart, lungs, and blindness, and Lucky's running sore and mute condition. But Vladimir's omission of "desire" in his remark may be a totally personal statement—genital problems trouble him throughout the play—and may echo the absence of physical or spiritual passion in the play. His omission of "desire" may reinforce the (heart)sickness brought on by his physical/spiritual condition. The play as a whole becomes a working out of hope deferred versus hope retained, the wavering resolve to await Godot and the heartsickness that that brings.

When Vladimir says, "What's the use of losing heart now? We should have thought of it a million years ago, in the nineties," he distorts time. He juxtaposes what might be called figurative language or slang, "losing heart" and "a million years ago," with a concrete date, "in the nineties". Again, when Estragon answers Vladimir regarding how long he has been unhappy, his eccentric use of verb tense in "I'd [not "I've"] forgotten" dislocates chronology, which allows him to gain some distance from the truth of his present predicament.

Dislocations, distortions, and misunderstandings of time fill the play: "The light suddenly fails [not falls]" and "In a moment it is night"; "It must be Spring. / But in a single night!" In answer to the question "Is it evening?" the following exchange occurs:

Silence. Vladimir and Estragon scrutinize the sunset.
ESTRAGON: It's rising.
VLADIMIR: Impossible.
ESTRAGON: Perhaps it's dawn.

Each of these examples demonstrates the asyndetic omission of causal links or logical connections that traditionally focus a statement toward a goal.[7] Although sections of Lucky's monologue exemplify asyndetic non sequiturs as well as paradox and concretizations ("[God] loves us dearly with some exceptions for reasons unknown but time will tell"), asyndetic omissions recur within seemingly comprehensible interchanges. When Estragon is asked if he remembers the holy lands, he replies, "I remember the maps of the Holy Lands. Coloured they were. Very pretty. The Dead Sea was pale blue. The very look of it made me thirsty. That's where we'll go . . . for our honeymoon." Although the comment may reflect Estragon's childlike sensory pleasures or his deep-seated hostility to Vladimir (discussed below), one's first response is that his reply is not focused on answering Vladimir's question. Again, the personalized response avoids the question. Estragon connects the memory of a color with past thirst and suggests, for the future, that they go to the traditional source of spiritual succor (the Holy Lands). Estragon is always aware of his fallen state.

Asyndetic thinking frequently has a poetic quality, although it is a poetry born of an entirely personal idiom. Words, independent of consensual associational meaning, become affective, like the rhythmical or rhyming sounds of a foreign language, as in Lucky's "Feckham, Peckham, Fulham, Clapham" and Estragon's "Macon" and "Cackon". Using approximations or "substitute words" is also poetic but, again, meaning remains private. Pozzo, who has difficulty breathing, says, "I can't find my pulverizer," when he means *vaporizer.*

Words that lack referentiality and are askewed from a logical goal often lend the dialogue an autistic quality: for example, when Vladimir says to Estragon, "Calm yourself," he replies, "Calm . . . calm . . . The English say cawm, . . . You know the story of the Englishman in the brothel?" The concretized anecdote that follows may (1) allow Estragon a story appropriate to his own hedonistic interests, (2) provoke Vladimir by alluding to his problematic genital ailment, (3) comfort Vladimir by distracting him with a joke or pun, or (4) allow the two, after their temporary crisis, to return to their set role playing. Although Estragon's story may serve one, all, or none of these functions, the only certainty is that it makes no clear, goal-directed sense.

"Clang associations" typify asyndetic poetic dialogue, uniting words on the basis of their common vowel or consonantal sounds. The following exchange illustrates how each speaker imbues his words with an entirely personal meaning. Estragon has mistaken Pozzo for Godot:

ESTRAGON: Bozzo . . . Bozzo . . .
VLADIMIR: Pozzo . . . Pozzo . . .
ESTRAGON: PPPOZZZO!
VLADIMIR: Is it Pozzo or Bozzo?
ESTRAGON: Pozzo . . . no. . . . I'm afraid I . . . no . . . I don't seem to . . . . . .
VLADIMIR: I once knew a family named Gozzo.

A kind of primitive poetry fills the play in its many sequences of repeated dialogue:

POZZO: What was I saying? . . . What was I saying?
ESTRAGON: What'll we do, what'll we do.

and

VLADIMIR: The tree!
ESTRAGON: The tree!

and

VLADIMIR: It'd give us an erection!
ESTRAGON: . . . An erection!

So, too, Lucky's definition of God's "apathia . . . athambia . . . aphasia" describes the limitations of God's powers, as well as the gratuitousness of His benevolence. But his stringing together of words, as in "running cycling swimming flying floating riding gliding cona-ting," may be motivated more by the sounds of the words and their rhythmical properties than by his intent to state that games or sports, like every other human activity, lead to oblivion.

The foregoing accounts for how proper names in dreams may be generated through aural, visual, or phonetic similarities. Some, like Godot/Pozzo, deserve additional attention because they take unto themselves paralogical and, at times, magical thinking. Pozzo, "made in God's image," enjoys being regarded with "fear and trembling." Pozzo calls his underling Lucky Atlas, the son of Jupiter, and Estragon mistakes Pozzo for Godot, not only because he looks like their imagined Godot, but also because the *o* sound unites Pozzo, Godot, and Gogo in his mind. Furthermore, the *o* sound and the shape of a well, *pozzo* in Italian, function as emblems of totality and nothingness—the conglomerative meaning of waiting and game playing, reason and unreason, the circularity of wish, as opposed to the actuality of Godot. Finally, the *o* sound, as mentioned earlier, represents Bion's goal of psychic wholeness.

Magical thinking is exemplified in the use of synonyms and the incremental modification of proper names. As words or objects are endowed with magical qualities, Pozzo's search for his pipe ("briar") transforms into a perhaps more hopeful search for a "dudeen," which becomes his desperate quest for his "Kapp and Peterson," at which point he is "on the verge of tears." Estragon and Vladimir's urgency to return to their set repartee functions as a guarantee against ill fortune:

VLADIMIR: Say something!
ESTRAGON: I'm trying!
VLADIMIR *(in anguish):* Say anything at all!

Beckett's logic would seem to be that game playing is, after all, ritual, and when ritual is invested with magical meaning, it becomes religion.

Concrete thinking, at the heart of primary process thought, has various manifestations in what are traditionally called abstraction or metaphoric equivalents, although the spatial gap (Jakobson's distinction between vertical and horizontal dimensions) is dissolved between the two parts of the analogy or metaphor. That is, the subtle distinction maintained in the use of *like* rather than *as* evaporates. Lucky is not a man who behaves like a beast of burden; he feels and is treated like an animal and is thus portrayed as one, complete with rope and a load to cart. Similarly, because Estragon is told that he and Vladimir are no longer tied to Godot, Estragon mistakes Pozzo for Godot simply because Pozzo holds Lucky on a rope. When asked if Vladimir is sixty or seventy, Estragon replies that he is eleven. Pozzo has great difficulty sitting because he concretizes standing as gaining (godlike or lunar) power: "How am I to sit down . . . now that I have risen?"

Because the unconscious is incapable of abstraction, primary process often transforms statements into pseudoabstractions or partially concretizes or distorts them completely. Estragon appears to understand Vladimir's "Let wait till we know exactly how we stand," but he fails to grasp Vladimir's next, contradictory statement: "Let's strike while the iron is hot." Estragon translates the metaphor concretely, first agreeing with Vladimir's initial statement that they wait, but then replying, "It might be better to strike the iron before it freezes." The sensual partner, who can never know how they stand (and who frequently totters), lacks any comprehension of the metaphor "Strike while the iron is hot." He says that it might therefore be better to act not by modifying their behavior in some undefined way, as Vladimir suggests, but by literally attacking the iron when, reversing Vladimir's sensory terms, the iron is cold but not yet frozen.

One of the most obvious examples of concrete thinking involves Vladimir and Estragon's relationship to Godot, a linking in which their wish is transformed into the certainty of their appointment. While in waking life it is mad to consider God in flesh-and-blood terms because God is a delusion as far as the senses tell us, in dreams, fears and hopes are enacted concretely, and one can thus expect Godot to be not like a father but, in fact, the father. As primary process articulates what secondary process analogizes, Vladimir and Estragon concretize the anthropomorphic deity as an actual flesh-and-blood person, Mr. Godot, a businessman:

ESTRAGON: What exactly did we ask [Godot] for? . . . A vague supplication. . . . And what did he reply?
VLADIMIR: That he'd have to think it over.
ESTRAGON: In the quiet of his home.
VLADIMIR: Consult his family.
ESTRAGON: His friends.
VLADIMIR: His agents.
ESTRAGON: His correspondents.
VLADIMIR: His books.
ESTRAGON: His bank account.

Yet like the traditional godhead, their Godot requires "supplication," and at one point they say that if they abandoned or "dropped" Godot, "he'd punish us."

That all of the characters suffer from somatic complaints is another manifestation of concrete thinking, as it simultaneously conveys their metaphysical condition.[8] Vladimir and Estragon, for example, project their psychological and metaphysical pain onto, fittingly, a boot ("Go-go") and hat (for the thinker, Didi). Another example of primary process's concretization of abstraction involves the dramatic transformation of Pozzo and Lucky. Assured of his direction in life and confident of his control over time, Pozzo, in the daytime, in the sun, has literal vision. But nighttime frightens him. At one point he advises Vladimir and Estragon, "I'd wait till it was black night before I gave up." Elsewhere, Estragon says of Pozzo's fear, "Everything seems black to him to-day." It is thus concretely appropriate that at his "recognition scene," when humbled and aware of his meaningless and arrogant endeavors, he experiences his dark night of the soul and concretely becomes blind.

In the concretizing of abstractions, objects or metaphors are treated as though they were literally the things they may be said to represent: for example, Lucky's putting on his hat before he philosophizes, as though it were literally his "thinking hat"; Pozzo's remarking that Lucky "can't think without his hat"; Vladimir's comment after locating Lucky's hat: "Now our troubles are over"; Vladimir's earliest efforts to gain control over his life as "he takes off his hat, peers into it . . . [and] knocks on the crown"; and one of the play's funniest scenes, the vaudeville routine in which all the confused characters rapidly switch hats. Sometimes these objects become highly personalized. Not only do Vladimir and Pozzo read the sky and light as though it will personally announce their fate, that is, when Godot will come, but the sun and moon come to function like physical extensions of their minds and bodies.

If, existentially, the individual is the measure of his universe—author, actor, and director—unconsciously, one occupies that center concretely as both subject and object. Thus speaking in both the objective and nominative case, Estragon is, on the one hand, affected by the moon, for when it rises it "shed[s] a pale light on the scene"; on the other hand, he says *he* is "pale for weariness . . . of climbing and gazing on the likes of us." One of the play's most moving sequences involving the personalization of time occurs when Vladimir and Estragon have the illusion Godot has arrived and their eternal waiting has ceased. For them, tomorrow has come at last: "We are no longer alone, waiting for the night, . . . waiting for . . . waiting. . . . All evening we have struggled, unassisted. Now it's over. It's already tomorrow."

At one point, Estragon is the only character who knows that the true measurement of time is internal. He correctly contradicts Pozzo's "I hear nothing" with "I hear something," and he does this by listening to Pozzo's heart. At the other extreme, when Pozzo believed he could control time, he took comfort in his "half-hunter," which he admitted was an instrument of "deadbeat escapement." By act II, however, Pozzo's blindness, like Lucky's bags filled with detritus—mementos of meaninglessness—has become an emblem of human evanescence.

SIX

"The key word . . . is 'perhaps' "

INTERVIEWER: How can you be so preoccupied with salvation when you don't believe in it?

BECKETT: I am interested in the shape of ideas, even if I do not believe in them. There is a wonderful sentence in Augustine. I wish I could remember the Latin. It is even finer in Latin than in English: "Do not despair; one of the thieves was saved. Do not presume; one of the thieves was damned." That sentence has a wonderful shape. It is the shape that matters.

Beckett's unique stage rhetoric, in keeping with the complex networking of total mental functioning, animates the play's every detail, propelling it into multiple transformations. Pozzo's chicken bones, for example, become the skulls, skeletons, corpses, and charnel houses that punctuate the play, haunting reminders of human destiny. The rock, tree, rope, hats, trousers, pipe, vaporizer, bones, coat, glasses, leaves, stool, and whip merge into a conglomerative object or conglomerative emblem, if you will, of achievement and surrender, hope and suffering—of the continuously assertive but futile act of waiting for personal verification and salvation, for a raison d'être.

If Beckett's treatment of objects is in keeping with unconscious, primary process thought, as he serializes objects as dream images of unconscious needs, his handling of them also underscores the existential dimension of the play. Beckett's objects are often familiar symbols of human endeavor and failure, like the eyeglasses, watch, pipe, and food basket that become useless to a blindman who finally understands his lack of control over time and space, as well as the arrogance of his earlier indulgences as a member of the privileged class.

In discussing Beckett's treatment of objects, as they reflect both conscious and unconscious levels of thought, another frame of reference may be helpful, for Beckett's presentation of them bears comparison with the work of Cézanne and Monet, the progenitors of the Cubists and Abstract Expressionists—all of whom explored the exigencies of the existential moment.

Beckett is known to have been deeply influenced by many painters, so much so that he reproduced their subjects and formal shapes in his stage designs. *Waiting for Godot,* for example, bears an uncanny resemblance to Jack Yeats's *Two Travellers* and *Tinkers' Encampment: The Blood of Abel.* The image of two lonely men on the verge of companionship or enmity, like Cain and Abel, was repeated in many of Yeats's paintings.[1] Beckett was drawn to Yeats's hoboes and clowns, to his recurrent images of a destitute and bereft humanity, as well as to his efforts to evoke the deepest recesses of thought. "Tapping the great internal reality," as Beckett put it, was at the core of Yeats's "incomparable" art, in "its insistence upon sending us back to the darkest part of the self . . . and upon permitting illuminations only through that darkness."[2]

As noted earlier, the Surrealists' fascination with the dreamworld had a powerful impact on Beckett. He shared their interest in the power of unconscious thinking, although he disapproved of many of their conclusions and artistic goals. He rejected their adulation of the unconscious, their certainty that revelations of the universal unconscious would create a "unifying mythos" that would better society and destroy the "rotting civilization" of "plutocratic materialism."[3] Beckett also rejected their facile dismissal of the rational mind and their naive glorifications of the unconscious, which they portrayed by juxtaposing recognizable and bizarre images in slick, strong coloration and traditional contouring, with paint applied in silky, *lichée* ("licked") techniques. This ultra- or hyperrealistic style was appropriate, they thought, in holding the mirror up to the singularly most important aspect of mental function, the unconscious.

In literature, Kafka modified this technique. In *Metamorphosis,* for example, he retained the Surrealists' meticulous goal of creating a hyperrealistic form, and his straightforward language, linear narrative, and traditional techniques of characterization provided him with a means of concretizing the inner world. Kafka portrayed, with the utmost clarity, a man as vermin, because this was the reality of his deepest (unconscious) sense of himself as well as the way the world had treated him. At the same time, Kafka allowed the speechless Gregor Samsa to process thoughts of normal, rational thinking. The power of the story grew from the conflict between the unconscious and conscious dimensions of Gregor's identity. Beckett required a form that would similarly accommodate the continuous interpenetration of both conscious and unconscious levels of thinking.

If, in his focus on the unconscious, Beckett was inspired by Joyce and the Surrealists, he was equally inspired by the Impressionists and Post-Impressionists in their efforts to depict reality. He could infuse his evocation of unconscious thought with their techniques of capturing the rational mind in operation—the logical mind in its quest to affix meaning in fleeting time. It is interesting that when Beckett first lived in Paris, not only were the Surrealists creating prodigious amounts of work, but the Impressionists and Post-Impressionists, particularly Cézanne, were also receiving major public attention.

Beckett's few stage objects and his sparse, repeated dialogue, the multiple evocations of the conglomerative effect, are not unlike the limited shapes that one associates with Cézanne and Monet. Regardless of their obvious differences, these artists, like Beckett, were addressing epistemological questions regarding the limitations of reason and perception in defining or fixing the reality before them, as well as the impossibility of attaining meaning in a metaphysical sense.

In their cylinders, mountains, apples, lakes, and flowers, Cézanne and Monet sought out the seemingly indivisible, essential forms of the world. But their eye was limited by the ceaseless transformations of their subjects, given the random processes of individual perception and external event: the mountain or cathedral as it changed from hour to hour and moment to moment. Everything was in the process of continuous change and often decay. Like Beckett's boots and trousers, their subjects were phenomenologically real, but the artist could in fact render them only at the moment of perception. Cézanne's asymmetrical apples, like Monet's water lilies intermingling with reflected water and sky, would transform before one's eyes in subtle visual slippages, as the observer, like the artist, brought to the scene fluid optical, intellectual, and psychological impressions. Fixing or stabilizing the image was impossible because only process could be captured. Cézanne's apples and Monet's clouds, like Wallace Stevens' blackbird and Virginia Woolf's Big Ben, existed in the moment of becoming, of continuously transforming.

Cézanne developed the constructive brushstroke or bunched color, color applied in patches without regard to outlined form, and often left in shapes, to borrow Lucky's word, unfinished at the contour. Monet worked in a different direction with *l'enveloppe,* the piling up of painterly textures to evoke a rich, vibrating atmosphere. Nevertheless, the effect of both these techniques was to overwhelm the spectator with the richness and continuously evolving reality of their subject. Where was the lily pond as it reflected its continuous interrelationship with the other—in the lake, in the sky, or in each?

With the use of *passage*, Cézanne reinforced the flexible relationship between space and mass, a concept that would assume singular importance to the Cubists. One could no longer say that mass defined space. Each defined the other, and each required equal attention in terms of pictorial definition in color, cubes, squares, and space. In short, the painter's focus was on the fluid psychological, optical, and intellectual mechanisms involved in perception, as well as the phenomenological instability of the external world. Suspending the laws of gravity by rejecting traditional horizontal and vertical distinctions invoked, in a sense, the juxtaposition of rational and sensory response, if not the new laws of physics.[4] With normative figuration, coloration, time, and space thus set aside, the fleeting quality of time present reflected the artist's existential search for nature's purest architectural forms.

One enters *Waiting for Godot* much as one enters a Cézanne landscape. Both lack closure, have roads that descend and ascend to undefined destinations; there is no beginning or end. So, too, Beckett's silences and multiple tableaux—characters frozen in a gesture or making statements like, "Let's go," followed by *"They do not move."*—function like the white, unpainted areas of Cézanne's canvas, which stand in striking contrast to his intersecting blocks of color. For Beckett and Cézanne alike, these formalized absences, the blank canvas, the tableaux, the silences, are like a tabula rasa. The spectator is invited to freely associate, to locate the space (the words) that connects floating planes (the busy activity on stage) and to move in personal time and space from volume to volume (in Beckett, from conscious to unconscious thought). The outsider enters the subject, compelled by the slippages of fixed meaning generated by the artist's juxtapositions of phenomenological, psychological, and existential time. Despite one's instinctive knowledge that finalizing the cathedral or lily pond is impossible, aesthetic pleasure lies in identifying with the quest, in the process of pursuing finality or denouement. One is continuously seduced by absence and potentiality.

"The air is full of our cries," writes Beckett in *Godot*—like the pure, unpainted canvas characteristic of so much modern art, whose subject matter conveys a sense of totality and absence, the promise of meaning and the reality of uncertainty, like the illusory meeting with Godot, the emotional and rational experience of the existential predicament.

The boots, which function prominently in the play, have a meaning or reality that similarly depends upon the context in which they are apprehended, including both the state of mind of the observer and the ever-changing environment in which they are observed. The boots are objects of the phenomenological world and major components of Vladimir and Estragon's life games, and in their emerging characterization—like Cézanne's serialized canvases of Mont Ste-Victoire and Monet's Rouen cathedral—they concretize the entire shape of the play.

In the beginning, Estragon appears exhausted from his bad dreams and unsuccessful efforts to remove his boots. "Nothing to be done," he says, and one immediately senses the contradiction of his comment and his activities. Although he continues tugging at his boot after making this remark, his very action, in the first minute of the play, reveals the ineluctable flux of time and space. On the one hand, the act of removing boots seems appropriate because the play begins in the evening, and shoes are removed before sleep. On the other hand, Vladimir and Estragon have clearly just awakened. Why, then, is Estragon preparing for night? If, at the start of the play, Beckett stretches time beyond rational comprehension, his point would seem to be that the function of the boots is relative. In Beckett's world, boots are perhaps the most *un*essential necessity for the existential voyager. That is, one would be wise in removing one's boots in the Absurd universe, where there is nowhere to go, no reason to act, and "nothing to be done." A bootless Estragon, in fact, would be properly outfitted for waiting. Indeed, the inherent contradiction in wearing or not wearing one's boots is appropriate, given their lifelong dilemma "to be, or not to be." In short, Estragon's first words and action camouflage his emotional and intellectual ambivalence about acting in a directionless universe; the boots are an objectified manifestation of "Nothing to be done" and " 'Let's go.' (*They do not move.*)". As in Cézanne's landscapes, time and truth are fluid: the foliage is captured in both spring and fall; apples ripen before our eyes.

In act II, Estragon enters barefoot, and boots are not mentioned again until midpoint in the act:

VLADIMIR: Where are your boots?
ESTRAGON: I must have thrown them away.

Estragon's relationship to the boots has changed dramatically since act I. Now he would juggle with them verbally, reinforcing, even more than in act I, his inability to either articulate his pain or to take the initiative to act. Rejecting the very ownership of the boots, he addresses them as though they were subjects of abstract, rhetorical inquiry and denies them one of their primary identifying qualities, their color. When Vladimir locates them—"There they are! . . . At the very spot where you left them yesterday"—Estragon disassociates himself from them:

ESTRAGON: They're not mine.
VLADIMIR: . . . Not yours!
ESTRAGON: Mine were black. These are brown.
VLADIMIR: You're sure yours were black?
ESTRAGON: Well, they were a kind of grey.
VLADIMIR: And these are brown. Show? . . .
ESTRAGON: Well, they're a kind of green.

They might just as well be arguing over the color of waterlilies.

In act I, Estragon's bootlessness was generally appropriate for a spiritually and emotionally homeless figure, although his continued efforts to put them on or remove them indicated a residual control over his life. Now, in act II, his hedging and fragmented logic expose his increasing emotional helplessness and ignorance regarding any power or control, internal or external. Like Pozzo's coat, which Lucky held for Pozzo and which, at one point, Vladimir wore but removed to cover the sleeping Estragon, the boots, as Estragon rejects them, become nonfunctional, like the whip, rope, belt, hat, chicken bones, clock, and pipe, and become associated with the couple's uncertain redemption through Christ.

Vladimir and Estragon had considered the boots as emblems of Christ in act I, and they also connected their fate with that of the two thieves: one saved, the other condemned. Vladimir provokes Estragon into admitting his identification with Christ, when he says of Estragon's removing his boots, "You can't go barefoot," to which Estragon replies, "Christ did." Vladimir continues: "You're not going to compare yourself to Christ." Estragon then admits his deepest wish: "All my life I've compared myself to him," and Vladimir must remind him that they have been born to nonredemptive suffering: "But where he lived it was warm, it was dry." Matters of warmth, dryness, cold, and wetness aside, except as symbols or concretizations of their emotional state, Estragon agrees that resurrection is unlikely because Christ "they crucified quick," and he has been suffering for a lifetime. For Estragon, then, the boot remains an emblem of the slow, circular process of waiting, which, in a mirror image, is reinforced by the accelerated suffering of Pozzo and Lucky, on their own time and spatial axes, with their own transforming objects (the pipe, rope, chicken bones, clock, whip). Beckett offers some help in understanding the boots when he modifies the statement by Augustine that he referred to in the interview cited at the beginning of this chapter: "One of Estragon's feet is blessed, as the other is damned. The boot won't go on the foot that is damned; it will go on the foot that is not. It is like the two thieves on the Cross."[5]

Also reinforcing the boot as a manifestation of the conglomerative effect, "boot" in French slang is *godillot*.

The tree, the first and last object on stage, also has fluidity of meaning. It oversees all the activity in the play and is an emblem of hope and despair, evoking associations of timelessness and change from both Eastern and Western traditions. Most frequently in the play, it is associated with the Garden of Eden and Christ's Crucifixion, Vladimir and Estragon's potential hanging site and their meeting place with Godot. Throughout, it is a witness to and reminder of the fact that with birth comes reason, and with living or waiting comes the inevitable fall into unredemptive death. It also becomes a reminder of the ultimate truth that the search for stability or meaning, as an emotional or intellectual reality, is the pathway to madness or, in Beckett's word, folly.

Monet, commenting on his quest to arrest the moment—"I am searching for the impossible"—said to his friend Georges Clemenceau, "It will be said that I am mad."[6] Vladimir and Estragon take Monet's quest and frustration to the limit. They repeat their commitment to await Godot at the tree (their search "for the impossible"), aware of the uncertainty of their appointment. And in despair over their folly in waiting, they suggest hanging themselves but remain standing at the tree. Their sense of futility is translated into the decay of the universe, including the tree:

ESTRAGON: Everything oozes.
VLADIMIR: Look at the tree.

The tree takes on such profound personal significance that at one point they identify with it. They "do the tree" in pantomime:

VLADIMIR: Let's do the tree . . .
ESTRAGON: The tree?
Vladimir does the tree, staggering about on one leg.

VLADIMIR: Your turn.

Estragon does the tree, staggers.

Then, still speaking as though they were the tree, they question their very being, their waiting for Godot, their assumption of redemption: Estragon asks, "Do you think God sees me?" Once again, although they conclude "Decidedly this tree will not have been of the slightest use," they remain standing next to it and continue their waiting. Beckett's response to Proust's comparison of a man to a tree is of interest. To Proust's "man is . . . a tree whose stem and leafage are an expression of inward sap," Beckett comments, "We are alone. We cannot know and we cannot be known." Beckett then cites another of Proust's remarks, also related to the tree: "Man is the creature that cannot come forth from himself, who knows others only in himself, and who, if he asserts the contrary, lies."[7] *Godot*'s tree, often stylized in human form, is at first barren, but it transforms overnight to bear leaves, a symbol of Vladimir and Estragon's transformations from despair to hope.

Closely associated with the tree as the site of both their redemption, that is, their appointment with Godot, and suicide are Estragon's rope and trousers, which function like blocks of color that sustain and break linear continuity. The rope and trousers also represent the precariousness of Vladimir and Estragon's commitment to wait as well as their fear of abandonment. In act I, after Vladimir and Estragon conclude that a branch might not bear their weight and one man might be left alone, Estragon plans to "bring a bit [of rope] to-morrow." But at the end of act II, still without a rope, they decide to use Estragon's belt (in fact, a rope, because it is a "cord"). The rope / belt / cord has already acquired a number of meanings from its earlier metaphoric and literal uses in the play. But Beckett's time present contains all time past. In act I, the rope indicated, metaphorically, Vladimir and Estragon's ambivalent allegiance to Godot:

ESTRAGON: . . . We're not tied? . . . I'm asking you if we're tied.
VLADIMIR: Tied?
ESTRAGON: Ti-ed.
VLADIMIR: How do you mean tied?
ESTRAGON: Down.
VLADIMIR: But to whom? By whom?
ESTRAGON: To your man.
VLADIMIR: To Godot? Tied to Godot! What an idea! No question of it. *(Pause.)* For the moment.
ESTRAGON: His name is Godot?
VLADIMIR: I think so.

Shortly afterward, they are more forthcoming about their connection with Godot: "No use struggling," "No use wriggling."

With the rope association in mind, when Pozzo, whom they mistake for Godot, and Lucky appear, Beckett writes, "Lucky is the first to enter, followed by the rope which is long enough to let him reach the middle of the stage before Pozzo appears." The taut rope literally demonstrates Pozzo's power over Lucky, as well as Lucky's pleasure in having someone give direction to his life. Once more, time and space shift, as if one were viewing alternating blocks of color and shifting planes. Lucky and Pozzo act out what Vladimir and Estragon have only metaphorically speculated about their attachment to Godot.

Beckett continues, "Pozzo drives Lucky by means of a rope passed round his neck," a vivid image that resonates with Vladimir and Estragon's potential hanging as well as with that of the two thieves. In fact, after Pozzo and Lucky enter, Vladimir and Estragon begin to examine Lucky's neck:

ESTRAGON: Oh I say!
VLADIMIR: A running sore!
ESTRAGON: It's the rope.

VLADIMIR: It's the rubbing.
ESTRAGON: It's inevitable.

In act II, when Pozzo and Lucky return, the first blind and the other mute, "the rope [is] as before but much shorter."

As a means of committing suicide, Estragon's fragile belt-rope is as ineffectual in act II as the tree branch was in act I. It has become just like all the other deenergized or now-missing objects in the play: Pozzo's pipe, whip, vaporizer, stool, and glasses. Ultimately, like Vladimir's earlier "bough-break" stratagem, Estragon's plan that they hang themselves with a cord is ludicrous: "They each take an end of the cord and pull. It breaks. *They almost fall.*" But as an emblem of their deepest wishes, it is revealing, for it indicates their realization that if they abandon Godot, they will surely fall, and, as they put it, "It's not worth [Godot's] curse."

As the play is about to end, Vladimir tells Estragon to pull up his trousers. That Beckett's last words focus on Estragon's pants as well as his cord, rather than his boots, is enormously important. Throughout the play, the boots, like Vladimir's trousers, have been associated with suffering and with the couple's frustrated identification with Christ. Estragon's final bootlessness—and the transfer, in a sense, of Vladimir's trousers to him (or at least the emphasis on Estragon's pants, rather than Vladimir's)—marks the beginning of Vladimir and Estragon's epiphany, each man's acceptance of his existential plight, after which they return to their assigned and protective roles. Equally important at this moment is Estragon's *voluntary* bootlessness. Until now, the boots have been a prominent object in the couple's mutual game of survival, but their absence at the end suggests each man's difficult acceptance of his sorrowful state, a barefoot Christ born to suffering without redemption.

In the last minute of the play, *Estragon's* trousers *are* "raised." Vladimir, back in character, speaks the words that Estragon, also in character, acts:

VLADIMIR: Pull ON your trousers.

ESTRAGON *(realizing his trousers are down):* True. *He pulls up his trousers.*

VLADIMIR: Well? Shall we go?

VLADIMIR: Yes, let's go.

They do not move.

Augustine's writings on hope underscore the play as much as his statement about the thieves: "God by deferring our hope, stretches our desire; by the desiring, stretches the mind; by stretching makes it more capacious. . . . Let us therefore desire, for we shall be filled."[8] Estragon's stretched, capacious pants, earlier "fall[en] at his ankles," are now raised, transforming Vladimir's "hope deferred maketh the something sick" (his conclusion, in act I, about his trousers, his condition) into "hope restored." If Beckett could say, "One of Estragon's feet is blessed, as the other is damned," it is not inconceivable that he intended the trousers to embody the same proposition.

As the play ends, the tree remains an emblem of the promise of Godot and the spirit of human endurance, of the careful balance between hope maintained and hope deferred, " 'Let's go.' *(They do not move").* For just a moment they have moved from "doing the tree" to being themselves, taking charge of their lives. Each understands that he is playing in thrall to an absent father in play that will resume tomorrow. Herein lie the seeds of the existential condition.

Much like Monet and Cézanne, Beckett's multiple reflections on recurrent subjects, like the tree, boots, rope, and trousers, capture each in its momentary phenomenological reality, while never reaching any metaphysical finality. All things can be seen only in the moment, and their meaning changes from that moment to the next moment, depending upon time, place, and the observer. Godot occupies a realm that is not only finitely infinite but infinitely finite, both intellectually and emotionally.

SEVEN

Staging the Conglomerative Effect

Beckett believes that there is an inevitable sort of correspondence between word and movement; certain lines simply cannot be delivered from certain positions and without compatible "actions."

Charles Marowitz, following an interview with Beckett

"NO EXIT": A BALLET

That Beckett conceived of *Godot* in symmetries of visual as well as verbal design is apparent from the productions he directed,[1] his notebooks and scripts,[2] and the performance instructions he gave directors and actors.[3] Just as he merged objects and characters to reinforce the conglomerative effect, he manipulated space to accomplish the same purpose. Beckett's notes specify, in remarkably detailed diagrams and explanatory commentary, the instances in which specific themes should be developed (for example, 109 instances of waiting), as well as how and where stage movements and gestures should occur. That stage design was of paramount importance to Beckett is underscored by his insertion of three pages of designs, notes, and cross-references in the program of the Schiller-Theater production.

Beckett's use of space augments his portrayal of "all humanity." When a character repeats another's gesture or occupies "his space," individual roles merge, at least for that period of time. Horizontal, diagonal, and circular movements convey a fixed, visual image to the audience, and when the same movement is enacted by another, the audience associates the first activity and its accompanying speech with the newcomer; identity is communicated through spatial location. For example, when the arrogant Pozzo enters stage front, right, and boasts of his worldly possessions, he seats himself at stage center. Nevertheless, it becomes increasingly clear that Pozzo may not be the master he appears to be and may need his servant, Lucky, to provide concrete definition to his life, just as Lucky depends upon Pozzo for sustenance and a vocation. Lucky, once a poet, has taught Pozzo about the finer things in life, so when Lucky comes to occupy stage center, a rare event,[4] and to deliver one of the play's most significant speeches, it is as though he has usurped Pozzo's identity. Pozzo, at this point, lies face down on the ground with his hands covering his head in a crosslike form.[5] Who, the audience is visually asked, is more beholden to whom? It is as though, to borrow two of Beckett's main props, one were literally putting on someone else's hat or shoes at a given place. Space becomes a means of characterization through what Beckett refers to as his "subliminal stage imagery."[6]

Location on stage becomes a repository of fragmented psyches: the loneliness, restlessness, and despair that accompany the process of waiting. In the end, spatial designations emblemize the unity of identity. An ingenious device that works toward eliminating the demarcations of fixed character, dialogue, and place, Beckett's "symbolic space" also serves to unify past and present as they are experienced in the unconscious. *Godot*'s space play is an integral part, as well, of his portrait of the human effort to survive the existential state. Fluid spatial patterns define the dubious quest for a central, fixed point.

Space thus becomes a manifestation and microcosm of the randomness of the Absurd world, as well as the disarray of the fragmented, internal world. Choreographing the quest for a psychological, moral, and spiritual center in his use of space, Beckett fulfills the artist's mandate, as he had defined it in *Proust:* that form and content be one, "the one is a concretion of the other, the revelation of a world." When *Godot*'s people and objects merge geographically, they join the chorus of past voices and nature singing of human desiccation—in counterpoint to the illusion of meaningful activity in mechanical time and place.

Viewing a video of *Godot* without sound is like watching a ballet. Space (like silence) clarifies mass (like words), and action is measured in precisely timed rhythms, with figures moving in emerging and dissolving triangles, circles, arcs, and chords. After Estragon (the earthy man who often sits by his rock or sleeps) stands to embrace Vladimir (on a vertical rather than horizontal axis, often standing by the tree and looking up to the sky), the couple disengage and restore their game by raising their arms in arclike shapes. In each of their six approaches to the tree, they perform arclike movements that contrast and complement each other. The moon rises in an arclike shape.

Circular movements evoke multiple associations, the most obvious being the circular act of waiting, during which nothing happens, and the well-crafted repetition of activities in acts I and II that demonstrate the act of waiting. Circles reinforce the conglomerative effect: immediately after Estragon says, "We always find something . . . to give us the impression we exist," Vladimir helps the tottering Estragon to put on his boots. Two precise, complementary movements follow their success with each boot: first, after putting on the right boot, they turn in a counterclockwise circle in ten rhythmically paced steps; then, after putting on the left one, they turn in a clockwise circle in ten identically timed steps.

These circles, in turn, recur in the shapes taken on by objects, like the belt, boot, pants, and rope that tie or break in connecting partner to partner or in offering an escape through suicide. As such, Pozzo's rope—connecting Pozzo to Lucky in their master-slave relationship and connecting Vladimir and Estragon in their contemplations of suicide—lies in a broken circle on the ground during Lucky's monologue. The play's most dramatic moments are enacted in congress with circular movements. When Vladimir and Estragon approach the blind Pozzo and deaf Lucky, both on the ground in a crosslike position, they make circular movements around them: first, a counterclockwise semicircle followed by a second clockwise motion that completes the circle. Vladimir's "To all mankind" speech also concludes with a half-circular gesture.

The circles reinforce Vladimir's endless "round" about the dog, with its focus on the grave: "Then all the dogs came running / And dug the dog a tomb." The vertical image of burial subsequently connects with many other activities, for example, Estragon's ditch, "the gravedigger" and "They give birth astride of a grave" motifs of Pozzo and Vladimir's act II speeches, and the Eiffel tower, at which Vladimir and Estragon were once successful and where they might at one time have committed suicide. All of these associations are processed with the same paralogic that reverses the letters in Vladimir's song about the dog and in Lucky's speech about God. The richness of this spatial poetry invites endless interpretation. Of the last reference, Vladimir's round about the dog that is continuously *to be* buried and Lucky's description of God, one might conjecture that it is God, created in man's image, who has died and who must, but cannot, finally be buried if the quality of waiting is to change.

Once again one thinks of Cézanne's and Monet's canvasses, as Beckett captures process, rather than permanence. Paralleling his characters' well-rehearsed words, which stand in sharp contrast to the pronounced pauses and silences between the lines, as well as their transformations in role reversals, stylized movements to and from the edges of the stage reflect process and evoke unfinished speculation and emotional response. Idea and feeling, via movement, both in a state of perpetual change, define the universal effort to cope with waiting.

Beckett directed that in the opening scene, the earthy Estragon play with his boot in a manner that would visually anticipate Vladimir's later activity with his hat. Both look at and play with their distinguishing possessions, but they do so differently. After two efforts to remove his boot, one unsuccessful, one successful, Estragon is instructed in the stage directions to inspect his boot. Vladimir later inspects his hat three times and, in keeping with his more tidy, rational identity, enacts a much more elaborate, tripartite ritual. First, he looks at the hat and shakes it. Second, he looks twice and touches the hat three times. Beckett adds, "Look, finger (i.e., running his finger around the inside band), tap, shake, look." Third, he makes seven movements: he looks, fingers, taps, blows, taps, shakes, and looks. At the core of Vladimir's elaborate ritual, his circular gesture of running his hand around the hat band serves to restate Estragon's initial helpless gesture of raising his arms in the two arcs of a circle when he says, "Nothing to be done." The impotence of human accomplishment is concretized in the dance of repeated shapes.

As Cézanne's apples, painted in the process of decaying, force the spectator to interact with asymmetrical and shaded ovals that alter and age during the very moment of perception, Beckett's characters, in their multiple efforts to gain a direction in life, similarly act out their lack of progress and underscore their growing helplessness, their "wasting and pining." Once again, the spectator longs for resolution in the spatial poetry, the shifting movement on stage, but the flux of mind function and absence of direction or meaning in life can be conveyed only in directionless movement. Comprehension, even if illusory, can be captured only temporarily. Process becomes an end in itself. The audience is invited to participate visually and intellectually in the substantive motif of the " 'Let's go.' *(They do not move.)*" refrain.

THE NOTEBOOKS

In the *Regiebuch* notebook from the Berlin Schiller-Theater production of 1975, which Beckett directed, he prescribed in a very legible hand the staging of *Godot*, as he had come to refine it over the years. Typically, pages on the right contain analyses of special problems; those on the left, his diagrams and notes. Many pages resemble a geometry text, as Beckett designates his actors' positions on stage, the directions they face, the linearity or circularity of their movements, and the cues for those movements. He specifies even the points in the play at which ad-libs can take place.

In Lucky's entrance, for example, he calls for an emphasis on the burden he carries: "Load: in R hand bag and stool, in L hand basket, over L arm horizontal coat."[7] Indicating how Lucky should set down and pick up objects in obeying Pozzo, he writes, "[He is] never a moment free of load except (1) to dance, (2) to think, (3) when fallen. Does not resume load after 2nd dance. . . ."

The play, as Beckett conceived of it, is broken up into eleven divisions and numerous subheadings. Beckett catalogues "Visual Elements," "Verbal Motifs," and "Audial Elements" and breaks down the visual elements, for example, into fifteen sections. The first six treat the objects and movements of each character: "Lucky's Moves," "Lucky's Think," "Estragon's Feet," "Estragon's Sleep," "Pozzo's Whip," and "Vladimir's Tree." The remaining categories include "Inspection of Place," "Divided Circles: Arcs and Chords," "Empty Crosses," "Approaches by Stage," "Wartestelle ['Frozen' Waiting Points, Tableaux]," and "Smaller Mime Actions and Gestures."

Beckett's detailing of movement is precise: he indicates how small arc movements should fit into larger circular patterns, and whether these should be clockwise or counterclockwise. Clockwise movements—for example, Vladimir's movement of his finger around the inside of his hat before concluding "Nothing to be done"—are intended to indicate the temporal realm; counterclockwise movements indicate an escape from the world. After stating that they have asked "nothing very definite" of Godot, Vladimir and Estragon move from the tree and past the stone in a large counterclockwise semicircle. Circular movements refer to both realms: Vladimir turns 360 degrees as he speaks of the muck. Beckett's instructions are so meticulous that he indicates when "little turns" are partial components of a single circular and linear movement. The coordinated arcs and chords that are halves of a divided circle and convey his characters' endlessly repetitive activities are analogous to their sitting, standing, speaking or singing, either in harmony or in conflict with one another. These movements are of particular relevance in this book, which focuses on the contrasting and complementary nature of roles that frequently reverse.

Beckett also sets the pace for rectangular, diagonal, or triangular movements and is especially attentive to each actor's positioning in relation to the tree or rock. Estragon "belongs" to the earth and stone, while Vladimir "is light [and] is oriented to the sky. He belongs to the tree."[8] Given these specifications, complex patterns of geometric movement reflect complex patterns of personal relationship. At the end of act I, the pair's "poignant ambivalence" about separating is indicated by Vladimir's walking in a curved line to the tree and Estragon's moving in a straight line to the rock, after which Vladimir follows Estragon, and a geometrical balance is reestablished. Little turns, two clockwise movements, are dictated at certain points as the characters approach the stone and tree. In the six times they walk to or from the tree, for example, three times in each act, their movements mirror those of their partner. For one of the characters, two movements are curvilinear, that is, arcs in little turns and arm movements, and one rectangular; for the other, two are rectangular and one curvilinear, with parallel arc motions. Similar instructions mandate their patterns of parallel movement to the stone. As explained by two Beckett scholars, "[These] contrasting patterns

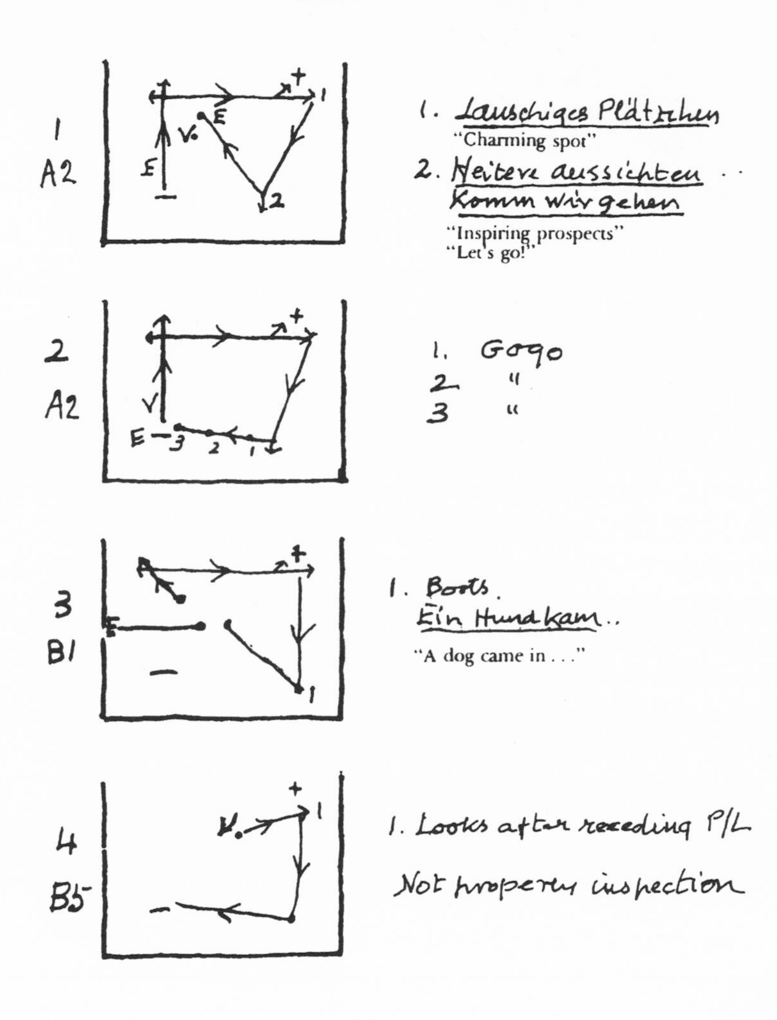

INSPECTION PLACE, *REGIEBUCH*, P. 73

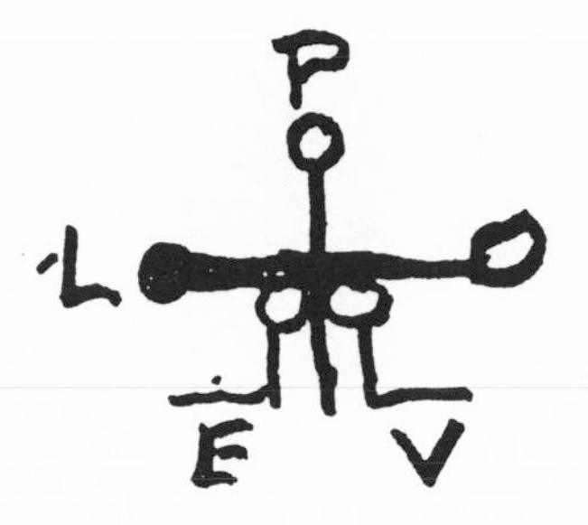

32

ELV

Bag B
Basket F
D
G
C
A

or

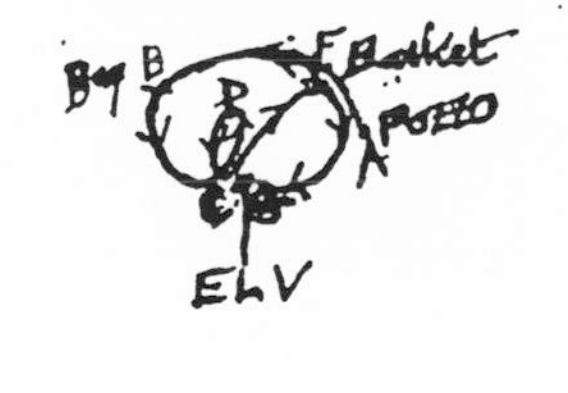

~~vielleicht [illegible]~~

← L

EPV

40

ihm entgegen gehen

A V takes E's arm for ← E breaks away for →

"to meet him"

3 Possibilities

~~1. E handles off when on again, V not off~~

2 Both " " " " " .

~~3 " off long enough for empty stage to carry~~

C Idiot V takes hold of E and draws him part of way to A. A–B backward B to shelter of V

B Du willst nicht

D Rühr dich nicht

D–V Den Baum kann man

after hinterm Baum V with E to tree

behind the tree

C Imbecile
B You won't
D Don't move
D-V Decidedly this tree

of movement connect the cardinal points of the tree and stone and define the boundaries of a closed, circular universe and exhibit the differing tendencies of Vladimir and Estragon."[9]

One of Beckett's fifteen visual motifs includes "Waiting," and he indicates that twelve instances of waiting should be underscored by twelve tableaux. These, he continues, are to be broken in very specific ways. In one, the tableau is to end as each figure assumes a gesture appropriate to his role reversal: Estragon's listening is to be balanced by Vladimir's looking. In addition, Beckett connects verbal motifs to abstract ideas, which he divides into "Doubts and Confusion," which includes three pages of specific instances of "doubts [of] time, place, identity, [and] confusion of persons." His examples include the general confusion about the appointment with Godot: Are they at the right place? Were they here yesterday? Was their appointment yesterday? Other instances of doubts include Estragon's forgetfulness of specific incidents and places, such as the Macon country; the couple's frequent verbal interruptions, like Pozzo's repeated "What was I saying?"; the questions about the boots and the exchanges over each one's misunderstood or unheard statements.

Beckett also tabulates the activities under his various subheadings. Under "Help" he counts "21 in all / 14 ignored / 4 answered / 1 attempt made / 1 not known / 1 on condition"; there are eight occasions of "Let's go. / . . . We're waiting for Godot." He provides his actors with a wealth of instruction: he notes the various times Estragon holds out his feet, walks in pain, puts on his boots (Estragon's problems are always with his left foot, reinforcing the traditional iconography of Judgment Day and of the condemned thief), as well as the structure regarding Estragon's three "sleeps" and two "drowses"; he indicates further that Estragon's position while sleeping is either near or removed from the stone.

The subliminal awareness of motif and movement will underscore, for the theatergoer, those sequences that are of special thematic significance in the play, like the line "When you seek you hear . . . , that prevents you from finding . . . ," which echoes the elegiac chorus of the dead voices that rustle like leaves. The senses of hearing and seeing and the gestures that accompany them—and the final image of the blind Pozzo, who can no longer find, and of the mute Lucky, who can no longer speak—are indelible demonstrations of the conglomerate "wasting and pining" of human deterioration. Movement, toward self-definition and an understanding of the universe, is treated literally and figuratively to indicate the means and end of waiting.

PERFORMANCE

> You should visualise every action of your characters. Know precisely in what direction they are speaking. Know the pauses.—Beckett[10]

> VLADIMIR: Let's wait til we know exactly how we stand [pun intended?].

While the Notebooks are fascinating in providing the specifics of Beckett's stage patterns, viewing the Schiller-Theater or San Quentin Drama Workshop *Godot* gives one an opportunity to more fully observe Beckett's stage design, which is often difficult to visualize from the notebooks.[11] One can also note stage activity that was not fully addressed in the notebook or that was implemented in an unusual way. Of major importance, most of Beckett's comedy is conveyed through performance. For example, in the midst of their confusion and despair regarding their appointment with Godot, Vladimir and Estragon play their line "Let's wait til we know exactly how we stand" with vaudevillian mastery. After two quick turns, they shuffle across the stage, side by side. Their steps are coordinated with Vladimir's singsong reading of the line:

Left foot/Right	L	R	LR	L	R	L	R
Let's wait—	til we—	know—	exact—	ly—	how	we	stand.

Similarly, when Vladimir and Estragon examine Lucky, they proceed, in unison, with alternating, rhythmical small and large steps. In their verbal farewell to Pozzo, funny in its mere repetition, they state their final "Adieu" very slowly, as "Ahhhh-doooo", and then move together, stage front, in measured, identical steps. When Vladimir presents Estragon with his favorite food, he gives him a thin, inch-long carrot attached to a long string with a bright green leaf on top, and says, "Make it last." Pozzo raises his wine with the toast "Happy Days" (a whimsical touch on Beckett's part, although he did not write that play until several years after *Godot*). The weary and limping Estragon picks up Pozzo's stool and, with the form and strength of an athlete, hurls it across the stage. On the occasions when Vladimir goes offstage to urinate, Estragon and, later, Estragon and Pozzo make loud, gushing noises on stage.

I want to isolate three sequences to illustrate synchronizations of movement and meaning: (1) the play's opening two minutes of busy physical and verbal activity; (2) the predominantly nonverbal sequence near the end of the Gospels discussion; and (3) Lucky's very brief dance. In each, pauses, like steps, are counted out in seconds, each in relation to every other one. Steps, like silences, could be measured by a metronome, which Beckett frequently brought to rehearsals.

The Opening

As the San Quentin Drama Workshop production begins, light gradually illuminates the tree, the road, and the two inhabitants on stage. The tree is a slim, graceful white arabesque, with a curved trunk and three curved branches; the road, in mottled blue tones, reflects the color and shape of the sky; a slightly darker blue separates the sky and road. Imprisoned in a universe they cannot understand, Vladimir and Estragon are dressed as quasi prison inmates. (Beckett at one time considered incorporating shadows of bars on the stage floor.)[12] Vladimir's too-short striped pants complement Estragon's too-large striped jacket; Vladimir's too-short solid black jacket complements Estragon's too-large solid black pants. The fabric designs reverse in act II. In the Schiller-Theater production, Estragon wears a beige jacket that matches Vladimir's beige pants; his dark pants complement Vladimir's jacket. In both productions, it is as though each were wearing the other's clothing. Yet Vladimir, the philosophical caretaker, who wears a tight, short jacket fastened by its single button is appropriately outfitted for a man who refrains from expressing his feelings. Estragon, soon to complain about his boots and physical needs, wears an unbuttoned jacket that is proportionally as oversized as Vladimir's is snug. His dress, indeed his corpulent body, is similarly appropriate, for he is the more sensual and uninhibited partner.

Estragon, shorter and heavier than Vladimir, sits huddled (Beckett's term) on his rock, downstage left; he faces the audience with his head down. The thin, tall Vladimir, with his back to the audience, faces the tree (in the German production he faces stage front) diagonally across from Estragon, stage right, rear. Following their initial silence and waiting, as Beckett instructed, the tableau is interrupted by Estragon's "listening" and Vladimir's "watching." Estragon then makes three guttural sounds, "ich" (described in the *Regiebuch* as a grunt or pant"), as he attempts to remove his boots. In the Berlin production, the sounds are noticeably brief but loud and well paced; they resemble a hiccup or belch, sounds one would expect from the more earthy Estragon.

Movements of the tall, slender Vladimir are so stylized, so strikingly mechanical in nature and measured in pacing, that it takes only seconds to sense the farcical or dreamlike nature of the landscape, whose first moving actor resembles a cartoon character. Vladimir's first movements are both comic and touching. Before he leaves the tree, he looks over at Estragon, looks back to the tree, and then turns around and walks toward Estragon in a pigeon-toed and knock-kneed gait. In the German production, as he walks he makes a robotic, circular turn and kicks one leg up behind in a jerky, almost semicircular motion. Occasionally, in keeping with his mechanized, clownlike movements, he puts his right arm behind his back and cups his hand upward. He may have a slight limp, but this is hard to determine because of his highly stylized movements.

When he reaches Estragon, he initially holds his left hand diagonally over his lower abdomen, as though he were in pain, and extends his right hand straight down at his side, making a triangular form. Shortly thereafter, when he begins discussing the thieves and the question of redemption, he looks even more like a sad clown or Chaplinesque figure. He bends more frequently with his knees and toes pointing inward, but now, he covers his genital area with both hands in the shape of a cross.

Vladimir's comic appearance, along with his stock comic exaggerations, will most frequently accompany dialogue about suffering. Implied already are the tensions in the conglomerative effect, a foreshadowing of the tragicomic, now visualized in gesture and motion. Exaggerations on stage in movements and mannerisms and seemingly sparse dialogue—anticipating the contradictions between conscious act and unconscious wish, between role assignment and role deviation that will follow—stir the audience to sense, in these first few minutes of the play, the unfolding of a comedy, but a comedy with a deadly serious edge.

The Gospels Discussion

As Vladimir and Estragon reach the last part of their discussion about the Gospels, in the Berlin production Vladimir augments his most somber question regarding personal salvation with comic hand routines, repeatedly cupping his bottom hand over the top one, in a rapid semicircular motion reminiscent of a child's game. Then, and in the San Quentin production as well, with his pinky down and two, three, and four fingers rapidly and alternately raised, Vladimir illustrates with finger motions his dilemma regarding the apostles, who considered, or failed to consider, which of the two thieves was saved: "One out of four. Of the other three two don't mention any thieves at all and the third says that both of them abused him. . . . But one of the four says that one of the two was saved. . . . But all four were there. And only one speaks of a thief being saved." The audience, now about ten minutes into the play, is even more involved in the unfolding tragicomedy on stage.

In the San Quentin production, Estragon gets up, in great distress. Wearing only one boot, as he does throughout act I, he limps stage left and assumes a lookout position, his hand in a straight, saluting position at his forehead. He then limps to stage right and performs the same gesture. He makes a slow, circular movement before walking to stage front, where he faces the audience and then turns around and walks up to stage left to join Vladimir, completing a triangle. The refrain is announced: "Let's go. / We can't. /We're waiting for Godot."

In the German production, after Estragon gets up, the directional cues are more emphatic. Both he and Vladimir face the audience, and together, in precise step with one another (one should be reminded of Vladimir's peculiar gait), they turn and face the tree. Vladimir briefly turns his back to Estragon, who then briefly turns his back to the tree. Estragon walks stage left, on a slight diagonal toward the audience, and Vladimir makes a series of body-bending gestures in order to reach Estragon's level. Generally, Estragon's turns are noticeably clockwise, Vladimir's counterclockwise, and they alternately walk on straight or diagonal lines. Estragon does not limp.

Lucky's Very Brief Dance, "The Scapegoat's Agony"

Lucky places his two bags on the ground; first, the bag in his right hand and, after a short pause, the bag in his left hand. With his face turned down and his arms at each side, he begins his dance, which lasts about ten seconds. He raises his arms in an arclike movement, creating a circle, and then lowers them and bends gracefully to touch the calf of his left leg, now also gracefully raised. In the German production, the dance, at first, is even more elegant as Lucky swings from side to side like a pendulum. As he arches his body upward, with his left leg still raised, the arcs of his arms disintegrate, and he frantically moves his hands in rapid, jagged angles. His fingers are extended, and he flails them above his head. As he concludes, his head falls and his arms drop to his sides. He then repeats the dance. Until the concluding, relaxed cadence, he looks like the tree in movement. His fingers imitate the arabesque shapes at the top of the tree, which looks like a stylized question mark with three arcs on top.

In the Berlin production, after the dance, Vladimir and Estragon stand at opposite ends of a straight line; the tree is the connecting apex of an equilateral triangle. The triangular design recalls the configuration of Vladimir and Estragon's earlier scrutiny of Lucky's sores and anticipates the geometric form during their imminent beating of Lucky. Time past and time present are visually contained on stage. Vladimir and Estragon then huddle together at stage left, dismantling the triangle into two broken triangles, as in the shape of a *K*; the shorter Estragon leans on a seemingly less frightened Vladimir. Lucky, although once a master of "the farandole, the fling, . . . [and] the jig," has now enacted "man caught in a net." Shortly thereafter, the once-agile dancer will deliver his frantic speech: chaotic fragments of a onetime poet-philosopher.

The most striking conclusion one reaches in studying Beckett's Notebooks or his Berlin production is that although the most important speeches are made at stage center—Lucky's, as well as Pozzo's and Vladimir's on time[13]—most of the play takes place away from stage center, with characters walking through or around the center, to and from a corner destination. All of Beckett's instructions emphasize that the stage lack a fixed geographical center, an appropriate conceit for a play about the absence of meaning in personal and cosmic terms. Concretizing his characters' predicament in the very space in which they seek closure is surely a tour de force—perpetually reducing geometrical shapes to fragments and then reconstituting them, as the characters act out moments of hope and despair in their quest to find a moral or spiritual center.

That the center does not hold is apparent in the multiple role reversals of each couple, which are accompanied by the formation and cancellation of their turns and counterturns and by their self-conscious and alternating movements from one part of the stage to another. All their so-called peripheral activities aimed at maintaining the status quo, to continue the analogy with the Impressionists, function like swirling colors that merge different spatial axes to eliminate a central focal point. As Beckett decenters his stage activity to spatially reinforce the absence of personal and cosmic coherence, he illustrates how, as in all human inventions, games of survival can be enacted only in directionless movement.

In the meantime, Vladimir and Estragon focus on objects that are off-center, the tree and stone, each one's only connection to the real, external world, although both the rock and tree hold out the possibility of damnation as well as redemption. The boot and hat are Vladimir and Estragon's only personal possessions, but these too afford only erratic satisfaction. Just as in the modern world, rationality and sense experience fail to satisfy mind and body, each object of the created universe is stripped of its prescribed function. Although one would like to consider one's possessions as gratifying and within one's control, they become as unsatisfying and mysterious in the order of things as one's belief in Godot. The riddle of an absurd world and an indefinable self would seem to be the only constant.

If *Godot* holds the mirror up to nature, its subject is the emotional finality of uncertainty. Connection with even the most modest of objects of the phenomenological world is as fragile and incomplete as the effort to understand the world and self. Physical movement—human life reduced to its simplest functions—is no different from waiting. Process is movement, but direction dissolves. There is nothing to be done in one's imprisonment in space. This is the emotional condition of humanity, folly given form, "the mess" expressed.

EIGHT

Crystallization of a Vision and Form

VLADIMIR: To treat a man . . . like that. . . . it's a scandal! (act I)

. . . .

ESTRAGON: Kick him in the crotch! (act II)

VLADIMIR: Let us do something, while we have the chance! It is not every day that we are needed. . . . To all mankind they were addressed, those cries for help still ringing in our ears. But at this place, at this moment of time, all mankind is us, whether we like it or not. Let us make the most of it, before it is too late!

Beckett is perhaps most ingenious in plotting his characters' relationships to one another as they share the common plight of passing the time, that is, of living in the act of waiting. In their speech and behavior, Vladimir and Estragon demonstrate the interplay of the rational and emotional components of human behavior. They may be viewed as two separate characters who interact on different levels or, in a sense, as two halves of a single self. In effect, one can view the interplay of rationality and emotion as interpersonal or intrapersonal. In either case, the more instinctual Estragon most frequently functions in primary process; the rational Vladimir, in secondary process.

In the Pozzo and Lucky relationship, Beckett again illustrates the mixture of conscious and unconscious language, but he also portrays another accommodation to the challenge of waiting. In this second couple, he exaggerates a dominant strand of mental and social functioning—one that is muted in Vladimir and Estragon—that of power and submissiveness. The interaction of the two couples exposes the precariousness of any role-play, of any attempt to balance the emotional and rational parts of self. In its dramatic climax, *Godot* exposes how the cruel underside of human nature may prevail at one moment, while at another, one may choose to engage in acts of empathy and kindness.

Throughout most of the play, Vladimir and Estragon act with a single goal in mind: to avoid sustained conversation about wasting, pining, and final oblivion. Their relationship, in which each plays a well-defined role, is essential to each one's well-being. It is as though they had agreed that if one player is the man of reason, speaking in secondary process, with the other, the man of feeling, functioning in primary process, they can minimize anxiety in the ordeal of survival. What becomes apparent, whether they are lifetime friends of fifty years or the divided consciousness of a single figure (fifty years old), is that the best-scripted efforts to surmount the human condition or human nature are endlessly precarious. They are as undependable as the order of the universe in which they operate.

Estragon, the more primitive, body-oriented partner, often speaks paralogically in remarks that have entirely personal associations and reflect asyndetic, concrete thinking. Vladimir, in many ways closer to Pozzo (as Estragon, in many ways, is closer to Lucky), speaks in more traditionally ordered, often abstract sentences, and his grammar and vocabulary are more sophisticated. Appropriately, Estragon/Go-go, with his boots, prefers that Lucky dance, as Vladimir/Di-di is drawn to Lucky's hat and prefers that he think. Estragon "stinks" from his feet; Vladimir, from his mouth. When not asleep in his "foetal position," Estragon blurts out his physical needs; Vladimir philosophizes or worries about his.

At the beginning, Estragon intentionally avoids answering Vladimir's provocative "Do you remember the Gospels?" He knows that discussion of the two thieves might, and later does, engender in Vladimir's mind a discussion of their own questionable redemption, a subject they try to avoid. So Estragon answers in a private, nonresponsive way; he connects the Gospels with their geographical origins: "I remember the maps of the Holy Land. Coloured they were. Very pretty. The dead sea was pale blue." To maintain their successful relationship and distract Vladimir from his somber contemplations, he concludes with the non sequitur, "We'll be happy."

Similarly, to disguise his acute disappointment when Pozzo reveals that he is not Godot, Estragon responds only to the alliterative quality of Pozzo's name: "You're not Mr. Godot? . . . Bozzo . . . Bozzo." When Vladimir counsels that he calm himself, his answer is once again private and seemingly incoherent, based on the sound quality of *calm* rather than on the logical meaning of Vladimir's communication: "Calm . . . calm. The English say cawm."

Estragon's lack of memory and inability to make time and space distinctions help the two avoid their most serious concern, salvation:

VLADIMIR: . . . the two thieves. Do you remember the story?
ESTRAGON: No.
VLADIMIR: Shall I tell it to you?
ESTRAGON: No.

Their roles or games may be well intentioned, but they are, after all, enacted in a world of mysterious design, which has given rise to them in the first place. Vladimir urges the forgetful Estragon to listen to his story because "it'll pass the time." But his story is about life and death, the two thieves, and the "Saviour." As a result, although the continuously forgetful Estragon tries to distract Vladimir with his "Our what?" and "Saved from what?," taboo subjects are at moments raised, and the game momentarily goes off track. Estragon says, "Who am I to tell my private nightmares to if I can't tell them to you?" to which Vladimir replies, "Let them remain private. You know I can't bear that." Some remarks are almost intolerable, especially when they relate to time and their meeting with Godot:

VLADIMIR: And where were we yesterday . . . ?
ESTRAGON: How would I know? In another compartment. There's no lack of void.

Until they recover a transitional cue, such as "charming spot," their consummate sadness and anxiety weaken their resolve.

As the play progresses, Vladimir and Estragon periodically lose control over their roles, and the game temporarily fails. Hence the multiple evocations of "What are we doing here?" and "Let's go." At these moments, if the two have been conversing on the same level, they may act angrily toward one another and, even worse, contemplate suicide. Inevitably, one or the other, in Beckett's words, always "pick[s] up the ball," and they return to their roles.

The beginning of the play establishes their assignments. The opening tableau, under Beckett's direction in the German and French productions, sets the two men in opposite postures; there is a long silence. Estragon is seated at stage front at his rock. He faces the audience, with his head down and his hands cupped before him. Vladimir stands near the back of the stage, with his back facing the audience. His hands are at his sides, his head turned toward the sky. The tree looks fragile, its branches shaped in arcs such as a child might draw.

Advancing with "short, stiff strides [and] legs wide apart," a debilitated Vladimir walks toward Estragon and observes his friend, who, exhausted by his attempts to pull off his boot, says, "Nothing to be done," a refrain always stated in the passive voice. In context,

Estragon is responding solely to his boot, since his assigned role calls for concrete thinking. Projecting his spiritual suffering onto his boot and foot allows his inner pain to remain concealed. Their game is begun, with the intensity of Estragon's suffering, the most important matter to him, in abeyance. Vladimir, as the man of reason who must also minimize their common condition, intentionally ignores both his own and Estragon's pain. He responds in an impersonal, logical, abstract manner. Apparently deep in thought, he avoids Estragon's concrete, personalized "Nothing to be done" with a seemingly casual, general remark, which he expresses more to the audience than to Estragon: "I'm beginning to come round to that opinion. All my life I've tried to put it from me, saying, Vladimir, be reasonable, you haven't yet tried everything. And I resumed the struggle. *(He broods, musing on the struggle. Turning to Estragon.)* So there you are again." Although communication on the subject of pain remains unarticulated, Vladimir demonstrates both the effectiveness and shortcomings of their role assignments. He understands and shares what Estragon is saying, but he responds to his own frustration in secondary process: he speaks to Estragon as if he were a philosopher, opining on the nature of human activity: "I'm beginning to come round to that opinion". Unlike Estragon, Vladimir can survey the past ("All my life . . ."), and he confesses that his lifetime of philosophical inquiry has left him where he began. He has tried to put aside Estragon's opinion ("Nothing to be done") by waging an intellectual, rather than Estragon's physical, struggle, a word that reverberates throughout the play. And this leaves him in the mental state of "brooding," which parallels Estragon's physical "exhaustion" after wrestling with his boots. Facing Estragon for the first time, his concluding remark sets Estragon back on track: "So there you are again." It is as though Vladimir were relocating his forgetful partner back on the gameboard. Estragon's response, "Am I?" and Vladimir's "I'm glad to see you back. I thought you were gone forever" end the first round of their game, with Vladimir abstractly mentioning their common struggle but in fact not comforting Estragon. Thus begins the rapid sequence of five or six rounds that structure the first few minutes of their play. It is Estragon's turn to take charge: with secondary process threatening to upset their consensual denial of reality, the pull of primary process emerges.

As Beckett gives form to this shifting between primary and secondary processes, he creates minidramas in which each character tries to be the other's leader, authority figure, even savior. In Estragon's preparation to replace Vladimir in their game and to play the "lead role," he "irritably" spurns Vladimir's embrace ("Not now, not now"), as Vladimir stands with outstretched arms. Vladimir, whose feelings surface after this rejection, becomes "hurt" and acts "coldly." When he asks Estragon how he "spent the night," calling him "His Highness," and a minute later, "Your Worship", his curious epithets—appropriate, for the moment, to how he feels about Estragon—convey his sadness and sense of diminution at Estragon's rebuff. The victory is Estragon's when he explains that he spent the night in a ditch, a safe enclosure, which elicits, Beckett specifies, Vladimir's admiration, the end of round 2, a point for Estragon.

A man with no memory or sense of logic, Estragon has no idea of the ditch's location. To Vladimir's "Where?" he replies paralogically in a contradictory manner, as the text indicates: "*(without gesture.)* Over there." When he admits that "they" beat him in the ditch, he brings up, for the second time, the subject of personal suffering, thus exposing himself to Vladimir's anger and predictable one-upsmanship. Vladimir's next generalization is one of calculated retaliation: an out-and-out insult because of (1) Estragon's rejection of his embrace; (2) his bragging about the haven where he slept; and (3) his reminder of personal suffering. Vladimir lowers himself to Estragon's ear and says, "When I think of it . . . all these years . . . but for me . . . you'd be nothing more than a heap of bones." Caring for Estragon, he continues, "is too much for one man." Back on equal, if not superior, footing with Estragon, Vladimir "cheerfully" returns to the more positive: "On the other hand, what's the good of losing heart now?" End of round 3.

As Vladimir continues, "We should have thought of it [losing heart] a million years ago, in the nineties," he slips in and out of Estragon's role, an example of the total mind in operation, as emotional responses intermingle with rationality. "Losing heart" implies both disappointment and death; "a million years ago" is both a slang generalization and reflection of the unconscious's boundless experience of time. His specific "in the nineties" tallies the fifty years of their relationship (or age), mentioned three times in the play. Essentially, Vladimir is saying that because they are no nearer to finding meaning in their fifty-year quest, they should have killed themselves at the start, "hand in hand from the top" of the Eiffel Tower. The tower is not only the site at which they might have committed suicide, but in another metonymic reference to Paris it refers to the days when they were young and hopeful: "We were respectable in those days". In primary process, the tower provides a spatial and symbolic contrast to Estragon's protective ditch, also a womb/tomb image: "They give birth astride of a grave", while at the same time it recalls a time of historic world success, as the Eiffel Tower was built in the 1890s.

His pain intensifying, Estragon asks for help in removing "this bloody" boot, and round 5 begins. He asks Vladimir if he himself hasn't suffered from the same problem, again projecting his increasing inner pain onto the boot: "Taking off my boot. Did that never happen to you?" Vladimir replies once more with a philosophical observation. Suffering, he says, is a daily condition, but he uses Estragon's boots for his generalization: "Boots must be taken off every day." He also reiterates the difficulties in attending to Estragon: "I'm tired telling you that."

Although they have successfully averted a sustained conversation about suffering, they undoubtedly understand one another and communicate on a nonverbal level, while remaining isolated in their assigned roles. Estragon has said, "Help me," referring to his boots and feet, and the dialogue following reveals both their isolation and their communication as these levels collide. Each partner will now repeat the other's words. Vladimir is first to ask the essential question:

VLADIMIR: It hurts?
ESTRAGON *(angrily)*: Hurts! He wants to know if it hurts!

Vladimir, acknowledging his own pain, responds "angrily," "[You think] no one ever suffers but you?" although the admission of his somatic or philosophical complaints remains generalized: "I'd like to hear what you'd say if you had what I have." The couple being dangerously close to a shared declaration of common suffering, Estragon begins the reversal of roles: now he asks the essential question, and Vladimir echoes Estragon's earlier words and tone:

ESTRAGON: It hurts?
VLADIMIR *(angrily)*: Hurts! He wants to know if it hurts!

Since the rules of their game prohibit a prolonged conversation about suffering, which seems imminent, they complete their exchange of roles at the beginning of round 6, and in the freshness of their new scripts minimize each other's anxiety. For each, the pain remains constant but in their altered roles it is submerged; they can thus pursue one of their calming routines:

VLADIMIR: Charming evening we're having. [specific]
ESTRAGON: Unforgettable. [general, for it assumes memory]

Sometimes, in coming close to forbidden topics, they risk losing whatever progress they have made in passing the day and return to their starting point, "Nothing to be done":

VLADIMIR: One is what one is.
ESTRAGON: No use wriggling.
VLADIMIR: The essential doesn't change.
ESTRAGON: Nothing to be done.

At such a moment, one or the other repeats his line or finds another strategy to get them back on track. When Estragon, for example, hearing Vladimir repeat his "Nothing to be done," senses Vladimir's distress, he affectionately offers him his preferred form of solace, food: "Like to finish it [the carrot]?"

Estragon, in his childlike, instinctive neediness, is at times the more comforting and pragmatic partner when their roles coincide or reverse. He feels the irrationality of Vladimir's suicide scheme and offers a valid, if illogical, reason for its unworkability. First, both are confused about who is the heavier man:

VLADIMIR: But am I heavier than you?
ESTRAGON: You tell me. I don't know. There's an even chance. Or nearly.

Then Estragon, presumably the irrational and heavier one, says to Vladimir, presumably the more intelligent and thinner one, "Use your intelligence, can't you?" And in fragmented logic and fitful phrasing, he explains to his rational partner that the scheme would fail: "Gogo [Estragon] light—bough not break—Gogo dead. Didi [Vladimir] heavy—bough break . . . Didi alone." Although he confuses their body weight—unless he paralogically equates weight with emotional security, rather than with physical substance—his thinking is correct for two reasons. If the thinner man hangs himself and the bough remains intact, the heavier man might break it and then be left alone. More important, Estragon emotionally understands the irrationality of suicide: if there is no reason for or purpose in living, there is no reason for or purpose in dying. The more vulnerable, irrational, body-oriented Estragon is, on this point, wiser than his partner. Because they can't decide who is heavier, in answer to Vladimir's "What do we do?" Estragon says, "Don't let's do anything. It's safer."

At another point, Estragon and Vladimir mix logic and paralogic:

VLADIMIR: When you seek you hear [not when you seek you find].
ESTRAGON: You do.
VLADIMIR: That prevents you from finding [seeking, not hearing, would prevent you from finding].
ESTRAGON: It does.

Their poetic, paralogical comments reflect their common purpose:

VLADIMIR: That prevents you from thinking.
ESTRAGON: You think all the same.
VLADIMIR: No, no impossible.
ESTRAGON: That's the idea. Let's contradict each other.

If Vladimir seems fixed upon a philosophical conclusion, even though it contradicts his usual position ("Thinking is not the worst") Estragon can distract him with nonreferential language and non sequiturs so that they can return to their routine:

ESTRAGON: Perhaps not. But at least there's that.
VLADIMIR: That what?
ESTRAGON: That's the idea. Let's ask each other questions.

Although they have each other as companions, each suffers an inconsolable loneliness. Their friendship, or psychological contract, as it were, is to cope with the gratuitous suffering of the human condition, to accept the reality that every man is a Jesus bereft of redemption. But accomplishing this demands that they "try and converse calmly." Otherwise, they will be reminded of all the "dead voices" of the past, the voices of all the others who were similarly stationed on the Via Dolorosa. The following evokes metaphorically Beckett's exquisite sensitivity to the connectedness of all things in nature, all striving for survival. Unlike Camus, who says that if he were a cat among cats, a tree among trees, he would be at home in the universe, unbesieged by useless reason, Beckett sees every particle of existence as striving for understanding. As his characters move from metaphor to the concrete, they unify the living and the dead, the vital and the inanimate:

ESTRAGON: All the dead voices.
VLADIMIR: They make a noise like wings.
ESTRAGON: Like leaves.
VLADIMIR: Like sand.
ESTRAGON: Like leaves.
Silence.
VLADIMIR: They all speak at once.
ESTRAGON: Each one to itself.
Silence.
VLADIMIR: Rather they whisper.
ESTRAGON: They rustle.
VLADIMIR: They murmur.
ESTRAGON: They rustle.
Silence.
VLADIMIR: What do they say?
ESTRAGON: They talk about their lives.
VLADIMIR: To have lived is not enough for them.
ESTRAGON: They have to talk about it.
VLADIMIR: To be dead is not enough for them.
ESTRAGON: It is not sufficient.
Silence.
VLADIMIR: They make a noise like feathers.

ESTRAGON: Like leaves.
VLADIMIR: Like ashes.
ESTRAGON: Like leaves.
Long silence.

These mournful expressions of need and anomie, in which both characters function on the same level, are the most affecting in the play, and Beckett frequently diffuses them with comedy. As Vladimir and Estragon, again standing by the tree, brood about their plight, the audience, like the couple, is diverted from despair by their concretized equivocations regarding the meeting place:

VLADIMIR: You're sure it was here?
ESTRAGON: Looks to me more like a bush.
VLADIMIR: A shrub.
ESTRAGON: A bush.

Elsewhere, their hopelessness is ameliorated when they change the subject:

ESTRAGON: Que voulez-vous?
VLADIMIR: I beg your pardon?
Ah! . . . exactly.
ESTRAGON: Que voulez-vous?
VLADIMIR: Ah! que voulez-vous, exactly.
Silence.
ESTRAGON: That wasn't such a bad little canter.

Their goal remains constant: to be "blathering about nothing in particular" so they can say, "This is becoming really insignificant." The juxtaposition of "blathering" and "nothing" is another abbreviated variation of the conglomerative effect.

Hope, for Vladimir and Estragon, like waiting, is a double-edged sword, for it is endlessly seductive and disappointing. Vladimir removes his hat (as Estragon shortly removes his boot), shakes it in the hope that there is something tangible or an idea within. He concludes by repeating Estragon's first "Nothing to be done." Then Estragon, finally pulling off his boot and shaking it, also paralogically illustrates the paradox of living or waiting. The acceptance of nothing is the definitive acceptance of life:

VLADIMIR *(takes off his hat, peers inside it, feels about inside it, shakes it, puts it on again)*: . . . AP-PALLED . . . *(He takes off his hat again, peers inside it)*. Funny. *(He knocks on the crown as though to dislodge a foreign body, peers into it again, puts it on again.)* Nothing to be done. *(Estragon with a supreme effort succeeds in pulling off his boot. He peers inside it, feels about inside it, turns it upside down, shakes it, looks to the ground to see if anything has fallen out, finds nothing, feels inside it again, . . .)* Well?
ESTRAGON: Nothing.

In the da capo movement of this diminutive scene from "Nothing to be done" to their parallel actions, back to "Nothing," both figures demonstrate concretely—in taking the hat off and putting it back on and in pulling the boot off, with additional gestures of turning each in different directions—that there is nothing to be done, nothing to be found, nothing to be revealed. The ritual of demonstrating or enacting nothing is the consummate activity of waiting/living.

Despite their role reversals and periodic displays of power, Vladimir and Estragon try their best to effect an egalitarian relationship, and they share numerous affectionate moments. They try to reverse actions that have estranged them. In one scene, paralleling another only moments before when Estragon rejected Vladimir's embrace,

Vladimir, a man of words, says to Estragon, "I have nothing to say to you," to which Estragon replies, "You're angry . . . Forgive me . . . Come, Didi. Give me your hand. *(They embrace.)*"

They hold hands and embrace frequently ("Come to my arms"), and then they hold on to each other, metaphorically and concretely, for life. They often refer to one another as "dear fellow" and are so grateful for the other's presence that they frequently say, "Thank you, thank you." At one point Estragon tells Vladimir to get up or he'll "catch a chill." At another, when Estragon tries to sleep, Vladimir sits beside him, covers him with a coat, and sings a lullaby. When Estragon's leg starts to bleed after Lucky kicks him, Vladimir "tenderly" says, "I'll carry you." During these moments, each is his brother's keeper.

In one amusing sequence they say,

VLADIMIR: You must be happy too, deep down, if only you *knew* it [emphasis added].
ESTRAGON: Happy about what?
VLADIMIR: To be with me again.
ESTRAGON: Would you say so?
VLADIMIR: Say you are, even if it is not true.
ESTRAGON: What am I to say?
VLADIMIR: Say, I am happy.
ESTRAGON: I am happy.
VLADIMIR: So am I.
ESTRAGON: So am I.
VLADIMIR: We are happy.
ESTRAGON: We are happy.

They incorporate into their routine even a discussion about their affection for each other: "Wait. . . . we embraced . . . we were happy . . . happy . . . what do we do now that we're happy . . . go on waiting . . .

waiting . . . let me think . . . it's coming . . . go on waiting . . . now that we're happy . . . let me see . . . ah!"

After they watch Pozzo abuse Lucky, they incorporate some of Pozzo's language into their game and play at insulting each other. They are meticulously polite, as they begin:

VLADIMIR: Oh pardon!
ESTRAGON: Carry on.
VLADIMIR: No no, after you.
ESTRAGON: No no, you first.
VLADIMIR: I interrupted you.
ESTRAGON: On the contrary.

Although they try to imitate Pozzo and Lucky, they have to cue each other about dialogue. And despite their politeness toward each other, the mere act of playing with hostile words exposes new feelings, and as "they glare at each other angrily," they seem less brotherly:

VLADIMIR: Ceremonious ape!
ESTRAGON: Punctilious pig!
VLADIMIR: Finish your phrase, I tell you!
ESTRAGON: Finish your own!
Silence. They draw closer, halt.
VLADIMIR: Moron!
ESTRAGON: That's the idea. Let's abuse each other.
They turn, move apart, turn again, and face each other.

At the conclusion of this interlude, their movement to primary process is apparent in the clang, poetic associations of their words:

VLADIMIR: Vérm*in!*
VLADIMIR: Abór*tion!*
↓
ESTRAGON: Mór*pion!*

VLADIMIR: Séwer-*r*at!

ESTRAGON: C*úr*ate!

VLADIMIR: C*ré*tin!

ESTRAGON *(with finality):* C*rrític!*
VLADIMIR: Oh!
He wilts, vanquished, and turns away.

The routine has accomplished its purpose:

ESTRAGON: Now let's make it up.
VLADIMIR: Gogo!
ESTRAGON: Didi!
VLADIMIR: Your hand!
ESTRAGON: Take it!
VLADIMIR: Come to my arms!
. . . .
They embrace. They separate. Silence.
VLADIMIR: How time flies when one has fun!

Pozzo and Lucky choose an alternative form of game play that highlights a less admirable aspect of human nature. Unlike Vladimir and Estragon in their egalitarian partnership, Pozzo and Lucky have a relationship based on domination and submissiveness; yet they too complement each other, Pozzo being the bully and Lucky, the compliant one. It is as though Beckett were introducing an alternative game to camaraderie—that of master and servant, with Pozzo, the well-dressed, egotistical bourgeois ("Is everybody looking at me? . . . Is everyone listening? . . . Don't interrupt me!"), and Lucky, his "menial" in rags. Unlike Vladimir and Estragon, this couple carries the trappings of the social world. They have wine for relaxation, medication in Pozzo's vaporizer, even furniture in the stool. Nevertheless, here too Beckett demonstrates that roles are fluid, that domination and victimization are as interchangeable as relationships based on primary and secondary process.

Pozzo and Lucky represent complicated mixtures of intellect and instinct, rationality and emotion. They represent the intrapsychic conflict every individual faces between instinctive and rational needs; in addition, interpersonally they embody the problems that develop between people in relationships when conflicts between intellect and emotion lead to strange and seemingly unequal alliances that, all the same, retain a psychological balance beneath.

The cerebral Lucky, a former poet and Pozzo's teacher, speaks but one time in the play and, in a mixture of primary and secondary process thought, delivers what may be Beckett's thoughts about human achievement, eventual oblivion, and the "unfinished" nature of one's comprehension of this cycle. Although, as Pozzo's "knook," he has a rope attached to his neck and endures Pozzo's threats "to get rid of him," he looks, acts, and seems to enjoy his role as a "miserable," "unfortunate" creature. After all, he has a partner who cares for his physical needs and who keeps him moving from one road to another, thereby giving not only direction to his life but a purpose, for example, to carry the bags.

If Lucky speaks only once (he utters an additional, truncated "On the other hand with regard to—"), his partner, Pozzo, the landowner, often expostulates at length in well-constructed sentences. In introducing himself, he flaunts the sartorial trappings and cultivated sociability of his class, and his clichés and goodwill are rendered in the language of secondary process: "Yes, gentlemen, I cannot go for long without the society of my likes. . . . The more people I meet the happier I become. From the meanest creature one departs wiser, richer, more conscious of one's blessings." He also boasts about the pleasures of sensual experience, although his language is offensive in its affectation: "The second [pipe] is never so sweet . . . as the first. . . . [It] makes the heart go pit-a-pat." Before his midday repast, he reflects on how "the fresh air stimulates the jaded appetite." He is speaking to Vladimir, who would prefer not to eat, and to Estragon, whose insatiable appetite must be content with a carrot or radish.

At times, Pozzo thinks and behaves in concrete, paralogical fashion. A forgetful man, he sometimes sounds like Estragon: "I don't remember having met any one yesterday. But to-morrow I won't remember having met anyone today," and "I'd very much like to sit down but I don't quite know how to go about it." A poet himself, his gestures often contradict his words. He says, for example, of the quiet night,

A great calm descends. *(Raising his hand.)*
Listen! Pan sleeps.

Pozzo projects emotional meaning onto objects and concretizes them: "You are human beings none the less . . . *(He puts on his glasses.)* Of the same species as myself . . . Made in God's image." Then he contradicts himself: "I am perhaps not particularly human, but who cares?"

Pozzo can relate to Vladimir and Estragon on their own specific thought levels. He accepts Estragon's statement that Vladimir is eleven years old, and because he understands that Lucky most often functions on an emotional, primary process level, before his long speech, Pozzo concretely says, "Give him his hat. . . . He can't think without his hat."

Most striking about Pozzo is how, while presenting himself predominantly in rational, secondary process language, he acts out his most hostile feelings: he puffs on a pipe as he pulls on a rope. His interaction with Lucky is almost always marked by a wide disparity between the humanity he tries to project and his less-than-humane actions. He strives to appear dignified and genteel, professing business interests and altruism—he is a cultivated landowner who is eager to travel and meet other people—but his greatest pleasure seems to be in verbally abusing and whipping Lucky. Pozzo acts out the most base elements of primary process. He degrades Lucky, calls him hog and pig, and in his acts, in traditional moral terms, is himself the brute he calls Lucky. At one point he reveals his misery in having to play this role of overseer to the dependent Lucky, whom he addresses as "My Lucky": "I can't bear it . . . any longer," he says. "I'm going mad . . . (*he collapses . . .*)."

Pozzo's and Lucky's mutual dependency is as essential as Vladimir's and Estragon's. Although Pozzo shows no interest in matters of salvation or damnation, which are of primary concern to Vladimir and Estragon, Pozzo depends on Lucky to bear witness to his existence and to be his scapegoat. Willing victims and victimizers, after all, need one another.

When Vladimir and Estragon are unkind to Lucky, Pozzo's response is both rational and socially acceptable ("Leave him in peace") and tyrannical and belittling ("Basket. . . ." "You're being spoken to, pig! Reply!"). Estragon's request to be given the chicken bones elicits Pozzo's rational reply: "In theory, the bones go to the carrier," but Pozzo's underlying self-interest is apparent. He needs someone to carry his belongings, serve him, and listen to his egomaniacal tirades. In short, the menial must be fed if he is to stay alive and serve. Although Pozzo complains about having to care for Lucky, he selfishly admits, "I don't like it. I've never known him to refuse a bone before" and "Nice business it'd be if he fell sick on me."

As disturbing as this relationship appears, the slave needs his master as much as the reverse. Pozzo says, "He wants to impress me, so that I'll keep him," and this is essentially true in that Pozzo gives direction to Lucky's life, even if it involves suffering. Godot, too, beats one messenger. Even as Lucky becomes increasingly debilitated, he facilitates his continuous servitude, deprivations, and punishment. He serves Pozzo his chicken and wine in the same spirit that he hands him his whip, and he weeps at the prospect of separating from his master. Pozzo understands Lucky's willingness to endure such treatment: "Let's try and get this clear. Has he not the right to [be free]? Certainly he has. It follows that he doesn't want to." He later adds, "The truth is you can't drive such creatures away." When Pozzo explains how Estragon should treat Lucky, he says, "To begin with he should pull on the rope, as hard as he likes so long as he doesn't strangle him. He usually responds to that. If not, he should give him a taste of the boot, in the face and in the privates as far as possible." Estragon replies, "And what if he defends himself?" to which Pozzo answers, "No no, he never defends himself."

That Lucky feels lucky in having a Pozzo is especially obvious when Lucky weeps at Pozzo's threat that he "waagerrim," that is, "wants to get rid of him," and again in act II when, with Pozzo blind, Lucky doesn't even consider escaping. Instead, he remains, and when the two finally depart, the blind Pozzo cries, "Whip!" and Lucky "puts everything down, looks for whip, finds it, puts it into Pozzo's hand, takes up everything again."

The meeting with Pozzo and Lucky is an important part of Vladimir's and Estragon's daily ritual. It is a diversion that allows them to depart from their two-character scenario. Pozzo and Lucky are playmates who provide them with a necessary distraction. In fact, the interaction of the four characters is integral to Beckett's revelation of the depths of human nature disguised by the games. The regular appearance of Pozzo and Lucky offers Vladimir and Estragon, as I said in addressing the conglomerative effect, the opportunity to help others. Vladimir and Estragon can and do choose to aid Pozzo and Lucky because, as Vladimir explains, "It is not everyday that we are needed!" They can extend kindness to those at their mercy, in contrast to Godot's response to them and God's response to Cain and Abel.

But the meeting with Lucky and Pozzo in act II also reveals not only the fragility of each character as he struggles to play out his role, but also the tentativeness of the roles themselves. All games are precarious stratagems behind which to hide one's awareness of the existential condition as well as equally precarious artifices behind which to hide one's baser instincts. Vladimir says, "It is not every day that we are needed," but adds, "Let us represent worthily for once the foul brood to which a cruel fate consigned us!" Pozzo and Lucky offer Vladimir and Estragon an outlet for the frustration and rage their roles have only suppressed. The cycle is this: game–altruism–cruelty–renewed altruism–renewed cruelty–return to game.

That Pozzo and Lucky are daily participants in Vladimir and Estragon's games, facilitating their psychological survival, is manifest at numerous points. Pozzo, for example, asks Vladimir and Estragon if he has played his role well that day: "How did you find me? . . . Good? Fair? Middling?" to which the couple reply:

VLADIMIR: Oh very good, very very good.
ESTRAGON: . . . Oh tray bong, tray, tray, tray, bong.

Pozzo replies, "I weakened a little towards the end, you didn't notice?" They continue:

ESTRAGON: I thought it was intentional.
VLADIMIR: Oh perhaps just a teeny weeny little bit.

Vladimir and Estragon's change in behavior is gradual. In act I, they are fascinated by this couple who function so differently from them. Yet Lucky's appearance and suffering do not initially disturb them, because on a primary process level they recognize his true psychological identity: he feels like a dependent, beaten, but cared-for animal and therefore is treated as such. They also accept without question Lucky and Pozzo's interaction, because feelings of aggression and passivity are familiar to them, even though they are muted in their own ongoing interaction.

At first, Vladimir and Estragon seem offended by Pozzo's aggressiveness: "To treat a man . . . like that . . . it's a scandal." It soon becomes clear, however, that they resent Pozzo's possessiveness of the chicken bones more than his treatment of Lucky. They dare not confront the man with the whip, so they turn their attention to Lucky. Although later, in act II, after Pozzo and Lucky become thoroughly debilitated, they will physically threaten both, now, in act I, they say,

ESTRAGON: What ails him? . . .
VLADIMIR: Look! . . . His neck! . . .
VLADIMIR: A trifle effeminate. . . .
ESTRAGON: Look at the slobber.
. . . .
VLADIMIR: Perhaps he's a halfwit.
ESTRAGON: A cretin.

The play reaches a climax in the second act, when Pozzo and Lucky, not Godot, appear once more. Vladimir's and Estragon's one-time fellow-actors can no longer provide a distraction. Now they are a living example of everything Vladimir and Estragon's games have tried to avoid: the reality of wasting and pining. With gameplay now impossible, the couple's despair and rage erupt. Any earlier displays of solicitousness are replaced with brutality.

As Pozzo is writhing and groaning on the ground, Estragon's first thought is, "We should ask him for the bone first. Then if he refuses we'll leave him there." Enticed more by the idea of power than of chicken bones, Vladimir asks, "You mean we have him at our mercy?" They become increasingly sadistic: "And suppose we gave [Lucky] a good beating. . . . fell on him in his sleep. . . ? Is he really asleep? *(Pause.)* No, the best would be to take advantage of Pozzo's calling for help."

In these, the most dramatic moments of the play, Vladimir and Estragon waver between the extremes of hurting or helping the couple, between the extremes of brotherly ambivalence. Vladimir's speech—"Let us do something, while we have the chance"—issues a cry for selflessness in the absence of validation: "To all mankind they were addressed, those cries. . . . But at this place, at this moment of time, all mankind is us."

Vladimir and Estragon's transformation, as noble as it appears, is not without its reversals. They do not attend to Pozzo and Lucky immediately; once again, metaphorically and concretely, they "fail," "stumble," "fall," "try to get up," and "fail" again. Vladimir says, "Help! . . . Quick! Give me your hand! . . . We've arrived."

They wake Pozzo out of his sleep but say of "this bastard":

ESTRAGON: . . . Kick him in the crotch.
VLADIMIR *(striking Pozzo): . . . Crablouse!"*

Reduced to hugging the ground and crawling like an animal, Pozzo "extricates himself with cries of pain and crawls away. He stops, saws the air blindly, calling for help."

Pozzo has collapsed from Vladimir's beating, and when they call to him there is no reply. Estragon asks, "What do we do now?":

VLADIMIR: Perhaps I could crawl to him . . . Or I could call to him.
ESTRAGON: Yes, call to him.
VLADIMIR: Pozzo! *(Silence.)* Pozzo! *(Silence.)* No reply.
ESTRAGON: Together.
VLADIMIR: Pozzo! Pozzo!
ESTRAGON: . . .
VLADIMIR: . . . We won't hurt you!

Since Pozzo still doesn't reply, they decide to "try . . . other names. . . . And we'd be bound to hit on the right one sooner or later." Estragon then "reflects" and calls Pozzo:

ESTRAGON . . . Abel! Abel!
POZZO: Help! . . .
ESTRAGON: Perhaps the other is called Cain. Cain! Cain!
POZZO: Help!
ESTRAGON: He's all humanity. *(Silence.)*

All humanity, it would appear, is both Cain and Abel, victim and victimizer, depending upon the role one is playing—and roles are continuously fluid and reversible. Thus Vladimir and Estragon compete with one another at the beginning of each day; Lucky kicks Estragon in the shins after he gives him a handkerchief; Lucky becomes the master, only because he is served by someone else. When Estragon pretends to be Lucky, and the actual Lucky "stop[s] crying," as Vladimir explains, "You [Estragon] have replaced him as it were."

Beckett's understanding of the human condition and human nature would seem to be expressed by Pozzo: "*(Lyrically.)* The tears of the world are a constant quantity. For each one who begins to weep somewhere else another stops. The same is true of the laugh. *(He laughs.)* Let us not then speak ill of our generation, it is not any unhappier than its predecessors. *(Pause.)* Let us not speak well of it either. *(Pause.)* Let us not speak of it at all." One moves imperceptibly and involuntarily back and forth from the role of master to that of servant, just as life hovers between tears and the laugh, between tragedy and comedy. One of the thieves was saved and one was condemned—in random manner. With joy and misery equaling one another in measure, the balance of life would seem to be a zero-sum proposition. Moral distinctions in such a random universe of laughter and tears are complex. The masochist who says, "Hit me!" and the sadist who replies, "No!" may lay equal claim to righteousness or indignation. Cain survives but bears God's mark, his curse and his salvation.

Beckett's familiar conclusion in *The Unnamable,* "I can't go on, I'll go on," resonates throughout *Godot,* as does Beckett's idea, repeated in the works of this period, that to have lived is not enough; one must talk of it. Hence, one continues to ponder the reason for living and the meaning of *human.* However, if human nature includes sadism (even Godot is sadistic in that, *if* he exists, he keeps the couple waiting and beats and may not feed one messenger-child), and if life consists of shuttling between joy and sadness, this, Beckett seems to suggest, is unsatisfying to the spirit. Despite the zero-sum nature of life, existence provides moments when strangers can help strangers, when kindness and courage can matter, however transiently:

VLADIMIR: We must hold him. *(They get him up again. Pozzo sags between them, his arms round their necks.)* Feeling better?

. . . .

ESTRAGON: He wants to know if we are friends!

. . . .

VLADIMIR: We've proved we are, by helping him.

ESTRAGON: Exactly. Would we have helped him if we weren't his friends?

VLADIMIR: Possibly.

ESTRAGON: True.

The exalting conclusion begun by Pozzo's speech and later elaborated upon by Vladimir is worthy of reminder. As Pozzo comes to understand the transitoriness of human achievement and the fact that action and material possessions grant only the illusion of power, his thoughts extend, for the first time, beyond himself. Pozzo becomes a member of the human family, and, as Estragon had mused earlier, may be a contemporary Tiresias figure, someone who gains the gift of understanding, if not prophecy—in *Godot's* terms, a Christ without redemption. Pozzo says, "When! When! One day, is that not enough for you . . . one day we were born, one day we shall die, the same day, the same second. . . . They give birth astride of a grave, the light gleams an instant, then it's night once more." For Pozzo, although the undefined "they" rule supreme, it is time for him, blind and infirm, to return to his ritual, so he pulls Lucky by the rope and announces, "On!" Estragon has already returned to his initial act in the play: "My feet! *(He sits down again and tries to take off his boots.)* Help me!" Vladimir and Estragon, who also continue on, immediately learn that Mr. Godot will not be coming. When they ask the messenger, "What does he do, Mr. Godot?" neither the characters nor the audience is surprised to hear, "He does nothing, Sir."

In the end, we are left with a view of human nature that is much like the one Freud described, and of the human condition, much as the existentialists defined it. With regard to the human condition, Beckett would seem to agree that we do not know if any ordering moral force exists or, indeed, if such a force does exist, whether its thrust is benevolent or malevolent. We are left with the inscrutable God of Cain's and Abel's universe. And just as no one escapes the precariousness of the human predicament, no one escapes the dualities of human nature. There may come moments in this zero-sum game when we can represent nobly that "foul brood to which a cruel fate consigned us," but if we do, we also know that the benefits of our service are likely to be dispersed by the interstices of time.

Is Beckett correct? Were the Freudians and existentialists right? Is life really a zero-sum game? and are "the tears of the world a constant quantity"? Psychoanalytic theorists have questioned Freud's view of human nature, and philosophers from the neo-Hegelians to the evolutionists have questioned the zero-sum nature of human activity. Were Freud, the existentialists, and Beckett merely representative of their time, spokespersons for the first half of the twentieth century, certainly the darkest era in modern times and, given the terrible technology humans themselves created, perhaps the most terrible period in history?

One may hope that the more optimistic thinkers on human nature will prove to be right. But one is daunted by the fact that Beckett echoes the likes of Sophocles and Shakespeare, no less than Genesis 4, and any optimism about human nature and the human predicament must, in the light of history's many dark ages, always remain guarded.

NOTES

INTRODUCTION

1. "Talk of the Town," *New Yorker,* 32 (May 19, 1956): 25; George Oppenheimer, *Newsday* 10 (April 27, 1956): 9.
2. Among the earliest interpretations, in the 1950s, see the brief Jean Anouilh, "Godot ou le sketch des Pensées de Pascal traité par les Fratellini," *Arts-Spectacles* 100 (February-March 1953): 1; on satire, Mercier, "A Pyrrhonian Eclogue," *Hudson Review* 7 (Winter 1955): 620–40; on Beckett and the morality play, Bonamy Dobrée, "Drama in England," *Sewanee Review* 64 (July 1956): 470–84; on religious elements, Charles S. McCoy, "*Waiting for Godot:* A Biblical Approach," *Florida Review* 2 (Spring 1958): 63–72; on the psychological, Charles I. Glicksberg, "Depersonalization in the Modern Drama," *The Personalist* 39 (January 1958): 158–69; on Joycean parody, Donald Davie, "Kinds of Comedy," *Spectrum* 2 (Winter 1958): 25–31; on comedy, Ruby Cohn, "The Comedy of Samuel Beckett: 'Something Old, Something New . . . ,'" *Yale French Studies* 23 (1959): 11–17; and on metaphysical farce, Rosette C. Lamont, "The Metaphysical Farce: Beckett and Ionesco," *French Review* 32 (February 1959): 319–28. For the variety of approaches in the early 1960s, see, on Jungian elements, Eva Metman, "Reflections on Samuel

Beckett's Plays," *Journal of Analytical Psychology* 5 (January 1960): 41–63; on irony, Ward Hooker, "Irony and Absurdity in the Avant-Garde Theater," *Kenyon Review* 22 (Summer 1960): 436–54; on the comic grotesque, Vivian Mercier, "Samuel Beckett and the Sheela-na-gig," *Kenyon Review* 23 (Spring 1961): 299–324; on the Freudian, Bernard Dukore, "Gigi, Didi, and the Absent Godot," *Drama Survey* 1 (Winter 1962): 301–7; on tragicomedy, William I. Oliver, "Between Absurdity and the Playwright," *Educational Theater Journal* 15 (October 1963): 224–35. Among the earliest books that discuss the plays, see Hugh Kenner, *Samuel Beckett* (New York: Grove Press, 1961); Martin Esslin, *The Theatre of the Absurd* (New York: Doubleday, 1961); and Ruby Cohn, *The Comic Gamut* (New Brunswick: Rutgers University Press, 1962).

3. Some of these early surveys, until the mid-1960s, include Jacques Guicharnaud, *Modern French Theatre from Giraudoux to Beckett* (New Haven: Yale University Press, 1961); Hugh Kenner, *Flaubert, Joyce and Beckett: The Stoic Comedians* (Boston: Beacon Press, 1962); Leonard Pronko, *Avant-Garde* (Berkeley: University of California Press, 1962); J. L. Styan, *The Dark Comedy* (London: Cambridge University Press, 1962); David I. Grossvogel, *Four Playwrights and a Postscript: Brecht, Ionesco, Beckett, Genet* (Ithaca: Cornell University Press, 1962); Frederick J. Hoffman, *Samuel Beckett: The Language of the Self* (Carbondale: Southern Illinois University Press, 1962); Lionel Abel, *Metatheatre* (New York: Hill and Wang, 1963); and Herbert Blau, *The Impossible Theater: A Manifesto* (New York: Macmillan, 1964). See also Josephine Jacobsen and William R. Mueller, *The Testament of Samuel Beckett* (New York: Hill and Wang, 1964); John Fletcher, *The Novels of Samuel Beckett* (London: Chatto and Windus, 1964); Richard Coe, *Samuel Beckett* (New York: Grove Press, 1964); George Wellwarth, *A Theater or Protest and Paradox* (New York: New York University Press, 1964); and Raymond Federman, *Journey to Chaos* (Berkeley: University of California Press, 1965).
4. Early work on literary and philosophical influences includes Edith Kern, "Drama Stripped for Inaction: Beckett's *Godot*," *Yale French Studies* 14 (Winter 1954–55): 41–47; id., "Beckett's Knight of Infinite Resignation," *Yale French Studies* 29 (Spring 1962): 49–56; Walter A. Strauss, "Dante's Belacqua and Beckett's Tramps," *Comparative Literature* 11 (Summer 1959): 250–71; Hugh Kenner, "The Cartesian Centaur," *Per-*

spective 11 (Autumn 1959), ed. Ruby Cohn, 132–41, and Jean-Jacques Mayoux, "The Theatre of Samuel Beckett," ibid., 142–55, and Ruby Cohn, "Preliminary Investigations," ibid., 119–31; Cohn, "A Note on Beckett, Dante, and Geulincx," *Comparative Literature* 12 (Winter 1960): 93–94; Robert Champigny, "Interpretations de *En Attendant Godot, PMLA* 75 (March 1960): 329–31, and Lawrence E. Harvey, "Art and the Existential in *En Attendant Godot,* ibid., 137–46; Northrup Frye, "The Nightmare Life in Death," *Hudson Review* 13 (Autumn 1960): 86–91; Judith Radke, "The Theatre of Samuel Beckett," *Yale French Studies* 29 (Spring 1962): 57–64; Germaine Bree, "Beckett's Abstractors of Quintessence," *French Review* 36 (May 1962): 567–76; id., "L'Étrange monde des Grands Articulés," *Revue des Lettres Modernes. Samuel Beckett: Configuration Critique 100* 9 (1964): 93–97; Calvin Evans, "Mallarméan Antecedents of the Avant-Garde Theater," *Modern Drama* (May 1963): 12–19; John Fletcher, "Beckett and Balzac Revisited," *French Review* 37 (October 1963): 78–80; id., "Samuel Beckett and the Philosophers," *Comparative Literature* 17 (Winter 1965): 43–56; Melvin J. Friedman, "A Note on Leibniz and Samuel Beckett," *Romance Notes* 4 (Spring 1963): 93–96.

5. See, for example, Jeffrey Nealon, "Samuel Beckett and the Postmodern: Language, Games, *Play,* and *Waiting for Godot,*" *Modern Drama* 31 (December 1988): 520–28; James H. Reid, "Allegorizing Jameson's Postmodernist Space: 'Waiting for Godot,'" *Romantic Review* 84.1 (1993): 77–96; James M. Harding, "Trying to Understand Godot: Adorno, Beckett, and the Senility of Historical Dialectics," *Clio* 23.1 (1993): 1–22; Una Chaudhuri, "Who is Godot? A Semiotic Approach to Beckett's Play," and Lance St. John Butler, "Waiting for Godot and Philosophy," in *Approaches to Teaching Beckett's 'Waiting for Godot,'* ed. June Schlueter and Enoch Brater (New York: MLA, 1991); "'This One Is Enough for You?' Indeterminacy and the Interpretive Tension between Text and Performance in 'Waiting for Godot,'" *Journal of the Comparative Drama Conference* (Athens, Georgia) 15 (1994): 73–78; "Beckett's Postmodern Clowns, Vladimir (Didi), Estragon (Didi), Pozzo, and Lucky," in *Fools and Jesters in Literature, Art and History,* ed. Vicki J. Janik (Westport, Conn.: Greenwood Press, 1998).
6. See Ruby Cohn, *Just Play* (Princeton: Princeton University Press, 1980); Jonathan Kolb, *Beckett in Performance* (Cambridge: Cambridge

University Press, 1989); Dougald McMillan and Martha Fehsenfeld, *Beckett in the Theatre* (New York: Riverrun Press, 1988); Lois Oppenheim, *Directing Beckett* (Ann Arbor: University of Michigan Press, 1994); Linda Ben-Zvi, ed., *Women in Performance* (Urbana: University of Illinois Press, 1990). Documenting the evolution of Godot through numerous productions and including a revised text is James Knowlson, *The Theatrical Notebooks of Samuel Beckett,* vol. 1 (New York: Grove, 1994). For studies of Beckett and music, see *Samuel Beckett and Music,* ed. Mary Bryden (New York: Clarendon Press, 1998); Lois Oppenheim, *Beckett and the Arts,* ed. Lois Oppenheim (Garland, 1999); id., *The Painted Word* (Ann Arbor: University of Michigan Press, 2000); Susan-Field Senneff, "Song and Music in Samuel Beckett," *Modern Fiction Studies* 10 (1964): 137–49.

7. See Harold Bloom's discussion of Beckett's "Sublime of Belatedness" in *Samuel Beckett's Waiting for Godot* (New York: Chelsea House, 1987, n.p.), 6. For two fascinating essays on the sublime, see Mark W. Redfield, "Pynchon's Postmodern Sublime" *PMLA* 104 (March 1989): 152–63, and R. Jahan Ramazani, "Tragic Joy and the Sublime," ibid., 163–67. Additional studies in this area include Paul A. Bove, "The Image of the Creator in Beckett's Postmodern Writing," *Philosophy and Literature* 4 (1980): 47–65; Yuan Yuan, "Representation and Absence: Paradoxical Structure in Postmodern Texts," *Symposium* 51 (Summer 1997): 124–41; Jeffrey W. Bowyer, "Waiting as Essence: The Irrelevance of Godot's Inconclusive Identity," *Language Quarterly* 28 (Summer-Fall 1990): 48–56; Albert Cook, "Minimalism, Silence and the Representation of Passion and Power: Beckett in Context," *Centennial Review* 38 (Fall 1994): 579–88.
8. I refer here to Joyce and his daughter, Lucia, who was diagnosed as schizophrenic. Lucia was a talented dancer and artist and a close friend of Beckett until her death.

CHAPTER ONE: THE FIRST FORTY YEARS

1. Alec Reid, "The Reluctant Prizeman," *Arts* 29 (October 1969): 68.
2. Beckett used to tell of "that dreadful man" who "asked me if I'd had an unhappy childhood, and was so disappointed when I told him, No, I'd been very happy and was fond of my parents." See Lawrence E. Harvey, *Samuel Beckett: Poet and Critic* (Princeton: Princeton University Press, 1970), 154, and Reid, "Reluctant Prizeman," 64.

3. F. X. Martin, *Leaders and Men of the Easter Rising: Dublin 1916* (Ithaca: Cornell University Press, 1967), 132.
4. Connolly, as quoted in Desmond Ryan, *The Man Called Pearse* (Dublin: Maunsel, 1919), 117–18.
5. Connolly's writings are filled with such statements—e.g., "No agency less potent than the red tide of war on Irish soil will ever be able to enable the Irish race to recover its self-respect." See Desmond Ryan, *James Connolly: His Life, Work and Writings* (Dublin: Talbot Press, 1924), and Nora Connolly, *The Unbroken Tradition* (New York: Boni and Liveright, 1918).
6. Jack MacGowran, "MacGowran on Beckett [interview by Richard Toscan]," in *On Beckett: Essays and Criticism,* ed. S. E. Gontarski (New York: Grove, 1986), 223; Dorothy Coote Dudgeon, in Colin Duckworth, "Beckett's Early Background: A New Zealand Bibliographical Appendix," *New Zealand Journal of French Studies* (October 1980): 60–62.
7. Paul Fussell, *The Great War and Modern Memory* (New York: Oxford University Press, 1975), 35.
8. In his widely read *The Modern Temper* (New York: Harcourt Brace and World, 1929), Joseph Wood Krutch observed, with unrelieved pessimism, that the dilemma of Beckett's generation was a consequence of no longer being able to sustain either unreasoning faith or rational doubt. He explained the new disharmony of thought and feeling: "Try as he may, the two halves of [one's] soul [could] hardly be made to coalesce, and [one could] either feel as his intelligence tells him that he should feel or think as his emotions would have him think, and thus he is reduced to mocking his torn and divided soul."
9. See, for example, Maurice Nadeau, *The History of Surrealism* (New York: Macmillan, 1965); William Wiser, *The Crazy Years: Paris in the Twenties* (New York: Atheneum, 1983); Noel Riley Fitch, *Sylvia Beach and the Lost Generation* (New York: W. W. Norton, 1985); Malcolm Cowley, *Exile's Return* (New York: Viking Press, 1961); Roger Shattuck, *The Banquet Years* (New York: Vintage, 1961); Samuel Putnam, *Paris Was Our Mistress* (New York: Viking Press, 1947); Sylvia Beach, *Shakespeare and Company* (New York: Harcourt Brace, 1959).
10. André Breton, "What Is Surrealism?" in *The Modern Tradition,* ed. Richard Ellmann and Charles Feidelson, Jr. (New York: Oxford University Press, 1965), 602.
11. *transition,* vols. 19–20. See also *transition,* vols. 16–17, 23–24.

12. *transition* 21 (March 1932): 105–45. Although Beckett was in London by this time, he continued to publish in Paris. The Surrealists—renowned for such statements as "The transcendental 'I' . . . is related to the entire history of mankind . . . and is brought to the surface with the hallucinatory irruption of images in the dream, the daydream, the mystic-gnostic trance, and even the psychiatric condition"—were affiliated with the newly planned *Variétés* (Breton and Aragon edited a special June 1929 issue called "Surrealism," which included an essay by Sigmund Freud) and with the newly revived *This Quarter* magazine. Beckett translated poems and essays by Éluard, Péret, Breton, and Tzara for the September 1932 issue of *This Quarter.* Surrealism gained increasing attention in various art forms. Films in 1928 included Man Ray's *L'Etoile de Mer* and Duchamp's *Anaemic Cinema;* Luis Buñuel and Salvador Dali were preparing *Un Chien Andalou.* The most significant art show of the year, "Au Sacre du Printemps," included Arp, Giorgio de Chirico, Ernst, Georges Malkine, Masson, Miró, Francis Picabia, Man Ray, and Yves Tanguy. Drawings and essays of Ernst, Schwitters, Klee, Man Ray, de Chirico, and Masson were reproduced in the many little magazines.
13. Lionel Trilling, "Freud and Literature," *The Liberal Imagination* (New York: Viking Press, 1950), 52.
14. On the war and Surrealists, see Virginia Williams, *Surrealism, Quantum Philosophy, and World War I* (New York: Garland, 1987). The relation of the Surrealists to war is especially interesting during World War II, when a group including Jacques Bureau became heroes of the Resistance under the name of their clandestine publication, *Le main à plume.*
15. In "Assumption," the unnamed woman is very much like Breton's mysterious woman, Nadja. She provides a good answer to Breton's opening question, "Qui sui-je?" as she represents both the "merveilleux" and chance. When she reappears and infuses new life into Beckett's young man, she allows him to experience the gamut of Surrealist contradictions: he can discover his own bestial and angelic nature; the savage and innocent potential inherent in both concrete and abstract experience; and the rewards and taboos, fantasied and real, afforded and suppressed, of the bourgeois world.
16. John Pilling, *Samuel Beckett* (London: Routledge and Kegan, 1976), 4.
17. Joyces's letters reveal his unwavering concern with the plight of the Jews during the Second World War. He made efforts to help one Jewish family, the Brauchbars, escape from Nazi Europe, and he privately as-

sisted at least a dozen Jews in their escape. He had always been interested in Jewish history, not just the gratutitous suffering to which Jews had been subjected—"the easiest of all prejudices to foment"—but its connection with Jews' (and his own) special regard for the family. He was especially proud to have "put Bloom on the map of European literature"; he even identified himself as a Jew in bondage during the First World War, when he felt like a prisoner in Zurich: "The Talmud says at one point: 'We Jews are like the olive: we give our best when we are being crushed.' " By this time, he had also dissolved his friendship with Oliver St. John Gogarty, in part because of his anti-Semitism. When asked why he left the church, Joyce would say, "That's for the Church to say." See Morris Beja, *James Joyce: A Literary Life* (Houndswell, England: Macmillan, 1992), 9.

18. Nora had been hospitalized for cervical cancer; his beloved daughter, Lucia, was suffering from schizophrenia, and his son had estranged himself from his father. Joyce's eye disease necessitated injections of arsenic and phosphorous, and he was given cocaine for his dizzying pain; his many surgeries resulted in near total blindness. He also suffered grave humiliation from his publishers' insults and neglect. And although profoundly devoted to his Catholic identity, he was considered a heretic by the church.
19. "On first seeing him, I thought there was just a touch here of the silhouette of James Joyce," said Nancy Cunard. Hugh Ford, *Published in Paris: A Literary Chronicle of Paris in the 1920s and 1930s* (New York: Collier, 1975), 277.
20. Peggy Guggenheim, *Out of this Century* (New York: Anchor Books, 1983), 144.
21. Richard Ellmann, *James Joyce* (New York: Oxford University Press, 1959; rev. ed., 1982), 6.
22. Ellmann, *James Joyce,* 188. See also Padraic and Mary Colum, *Our Friend James Joyce* (Garden City: Doubleday, 1958), 88, and Curran, *Joyce Remembered* (London: Oxford University Press, 1968), 88. He enjoyed a "good burlesque" and was always ripe for a good "leg-pull." His humor was "altogether unforced and boyish."
23. Ellmann, *James Joyce,* 546.
24. Ibid., 436.
25. Cited by Enoch Brater, *why beckett* (New York: Thames and Hudson, 1989), 28.

26. Quoted in Gordon S. Armstrong, *Samuel Beckett, W. B. Yeats, and Jack Yeats* (Lewisburg, Pa: Bucknell University Press, 1990), 165.
27. Quoted in Hilary Pyle, *Jack B. Yeats* (London: Routledge and Kegan Paul, 1970), 136.
28. Samuel Beckett, "Hommage à Jack B. Yeats," *Les Lettres Nouvelles* (April 1954): 619–20. Beckett exalted Yeats as one of the most important of all painters. He saw how, as in all great art, Yeats's smallest passages were charged with human significance and was intrigued by Yeats's artistic understanding of how experience exists only as a measure of individual perception. In the late, great *Tinkers' Encampment—The Blood of Abel,* the world is a temporary camping ground. Beckett's use of this image will be discussed in chapter 6.
29. According to Ruby Cohn, *Back to Beckett* (Princeton: Princeton University Press, 1973), vii. See also Vivian Mercier, *Beckett/Beckett* (New York: Oxford University Press), 31, and Linda Ben-Zvi, *Beckett* (Boston: Twayne Publishers, 1986), n.p. Pilling and Harvey, on the other hand, speak of Beckett's two years in London from 1933 to 1935. See Pilling, *Samuel Beckett,* 8, and Harvey, *Beckett: Poet and Critic,* 170.
30. Fletcher, *The Novels of Beckett,* 38.
31. Quoted in Cohn, *Back to Beckett,* ix.
32. Richard Ellmann, *Samuel Beckett: Nayman of Noland* (Washington, D.C.: Library of Congress, 1986), 10. Beckett's longtime friends Dr. and Mrs. Gottfried Büttner discussed this with me, April 9, 1992. From 1933 to 1939, the Nazis made no effort to conceal their activities. See, for example, *The Times,* Sept. 11, 1935; on the book burnings, May 11, 1933.
33. In *The Bookman* 87 (Christmas 1934), he published several pieces: "Ex Cathezra," a review of Pound's *Make It New,* 10; "Papini's Dante," a review of *Dante Vico* by G. Papini, 14; and a discussion of Sean O'Casey's *Windfalls,* "The Essential and the Incidental," 111. His review of J. B. Leishmann's translation of Rilke's poetry appeared in *The Criterion* 13 (1934): 705–07. *Dublin Magazine* 9 (July-Sept. 1934) included reviews of McGreevy's poetry (79–80) and Jack B. Yeats's novel *The Amaranthus* (80–81).
34. *Murphy* (London: Routledge, 1938); *More Pricks than Kicks* (London: Chatto and Windus, 1934); *Echo's Bones and Other Precipitates* (Paris: Europa Press, 1935). He also published both the story "A Case in a Thousand" and the article "Recent Irish Poets" (signed as Andrew Bellis) in *The Bookman* 76 (August 1934): 235–36, and the poems

"Home Olga," *Contempo* (February 15, 1934): 3, and "Gnome," *Dublin Magazine* 9 (July-Sept. 1934): 8.

35. Paul C. Ray, *The Surrealist Movement in England* (Ithaca: Cornell University Press: 1971), 146.
36. Patou was particularly concerned with adapting Christian, specifically Anglican, doctrine to the changing intellectual currents of the modern age. Bion's texts are also sprinkled with references to Kant. See H. J. Patou, *The Moral Law, or Kant's Groundwork of the Metaphysic of Morals* (London: Hutchinson University, n.d.); id., *In Defense of Reason* (London: Heinemann, 1951); id., *The Categorical Imperative: A Study in Kant's Moral Philosophy* (Chicago: Chicago University Press, 1948); id., *The Modern Predicament: A Study in the Philosophy of Religion* (New York: Macmillan, 1955).
37. In some of his works, he uses only the Greek letters; in others, he translates them. See W. R. Bion, *Learning from Experience* (New York: Basic Books, 1962); id., *Elements of Psycho-Analysis* (New York: Basic Books, 1963).
38. In the introduction to *Second Thoughts: Selected Papers on Psycho-Analysis* (London: Heinemann, 1967), Bion continued to explain that the content of dreams was neither pathological nor regressive. It could indicate things to come and could be integrative. Like Otto Rank, Bion believed that dreams could be even preverbal and prenatal.
39. See Bion, *Second Thoughts*, 5–6, 24–33, 38–42, and chap. 8.
40. "The patient who cannot dream cannot go to sleep and cannot wake up. Hence the peculiar condition seen clinically when the psychotic patient behaves as if he were in precisely this state." Bion, *Learning from Experience*, 51.
41. Bion, *Second Thoughts*, 36ff.
42. MacGowran, "MacGowran on Beckett," in *On Beckett: Essays and Criticism*, 223.
43. Like the period Beckett spent in London, the dates of this trip are reported differently. Cohn, *Back to Beckett*, ix; Mercier, *Beckett/Beckett*, 31; Ben-Zvi, *Beckett*, n.p.; and Deirdre Bair, *Samuel Beckett* (Harcourt Brace Jovanovich, 1978), 241ff., place Beckett in Germany from late 1936 until the middle of 1937. Pilling, *Samuel Beckett*, 8, and Harvey, *Beckett: Poet and Critic*, 170, date the trip between 1935 and 1936. The publication of Beckett's letters may resolve these differences.
44. From Gottfried Büttner, "Some Aspects of Beckett's Cultural Rela-

tions with Germany," a paper presented to the "Beckett and Biography" meeting at the Samuel Beckett Festival in The Hague, April 9, 1992, which I chaired. My quotations are from a photocopy, courtesy of the author.

45. Anna Balakian, *Surrealism* (New York: Noonday Press, 1959), 103.
46. John Hohenberg, *Free Press/Free People* (New York: New York University Press, 1971), 241–42, and John Desmond, *Crisis and Conflict* (Iowa City: University of Iowa Press, 1980), 405.
47. Ben-Zvi, *Beckett*, 15.
48. *Murphy* would finally be published by Routledge in 1938.
49. He also published "Ooftish" and "Denis Devlin," a review of Devlin's *Intercessions*, in *transition* 27 (April-May 1938): 33, 289–94, respectively.
50. Under suspicion, Suzanne was once followed back to their apartment; although the Gestapo saw the book on a table, with Beckett's copious annotations, they did not arrest her.
51. See M. R. D. Foot, *SOE in France* (London: Paul Elek, 1973); id., *SOE: An Outline History* (London: BBC, 1984). Generally of interest, see E. H. Cookridge, *Set Europe Ablaze* (London: Pan Books, 1965); id., *They Came from the Sky* (New York: Thomas Y. Crowell, 1967); Henri Michel, *Histoire de la Résistance en France* (Universitaires de France, 1972); Frida Knight, *The French Resistance* (London: Laurence and Wishart, 1975); M. R. D. Foot, *European Resistance to Nazism 1940–1945* (New York: McGraw-Hill, 1977); Claude Chambard, *The Macquis*, trans. Elaine P. Halperin (Indianapolis: Bobbs Merrill, 1970); Christian Durandet, *Les Maquis de Provence* (Paris: Editions France-Empire, 1974).
52. Michel, *Histoire de la Résistance*, 32.
53. Foot, *SOE: An Outline History*, 319.
54. Kathleen McGrory and John Unterecker, "Interview with Jack MacGowran," in *Yeats, Joyce, Beckett: New Light on Three Modern Irish Writers*, ed. Kathleen McGrory and John Unterecker (Lewisburg, Pa.,: Bucknell University Press, 1976), 173–74.
55. Laurence Wylie, *Village in the Vauclause* (Cambridge: Harvard University Press, 1974); id., "Roussillon '87: Returning to the Village in the Vauclause," *French Politics and Society* 7 (Spring 1989): 1–26.
56. In 1935, Francois Morénas founded the first youth village for nonconformists here, which he named Régain.
57. Francis Berjot, in *Roussillon: Le Temps Retrouvé*, makes reference to Beckett's warm treatment by the villagers, 75, and their pleasure at

Beckett's reference in *Godot* to Roussillon: "We worked in the harvest at Bonnelly's farm in Roussillon. . . . Everything is red down there."

58. James Knowlson, *Beckett: An Exhibition* (London: Turret, 1976), 44.
59. I refer to Wylie's interview with the villagers as well as to statements made by others who were in hiding there, including Beckett's artist friend and his wife, Henri and Josette Hayden.
60. Fletcher, *The Novels of Beckett*, 59, and Harvey, *Beckett: Poet and Critic*, 222.
61. Personal conversation, May 19, 1992. Since most of the cultural, economic, and demographic information on Roussillon during the war derives from Wiley, in conversation or correspondence, most of the citations refer to other sources (also derivative from *Village*).
62. On one occasion, the maquis learned that the Germans were sending a column to the area. They also knew that the only way to get from one side of the Lubéron mountains to the other was through the narrow Combe passage, a one-hundred-yard road winding through the rock. The maquis waited on top of the hills, and when the Germans reached the middle of this narrow path, they dropped ammunition and destroyed the column. They were never caught.
63. See "The IRA and the Origins of SOE," in *War in Society*, 155. Foot even compares Collins to France's legendary Jean Moulin, a former Chartres prefect, who had begun his Resistance activities at a farm near Avignon the year before Beckett arrived.
64. The fact that Beckett received the Croix de Guerre reinforces the notion that he worked for the SOE, since de Gaulle created the Ordre de la libération specifically, but not entirely, for the Free French. See Robert Werlich, *Orders and Decorations of All Nations* (Washington, D.C.: Quaker Press, 1974), 134; "Medals," *Encyclopedia Brittanica*, 1973 ed., 64; and Guido Rosignoli, *Ribbons of Orders, Decorations and Medals* (New York, Arco Publishing, 1977), 86.
65. Reid, "The Reluctant Prizeman," 68.
66. Wiley, in personal conversation, May 16, 1992.
67. Personal correspondence, August 2, 1992.
68. See especially the *Times* (London) from July 4–20 to July 24–26, particularly the photos of July 14, 1944, and the *Irish Times*, July 4, 5, 19, 27, 1944; all are front page articles.
69. As cited in Eoin O'Brien, *The Beckett Country* (New York: Riverrun Press, 1986), 327.

70. Ibid., 333–37, says, "It is unknown if the broadcast took place." He also publishes it in full from a typescript signed by Beckett. Others report that the broadcast did occur: Brater, *why beckett,* 44; Dougald McMillan, "Beckett at Forty: The Capital of the Ruins and Saint-Lō," in *As No Other Dare Fail,* 73–76, and John P. Harrington, *The Irish Beckett* (Syracuse: Syracuse University Press, 1991), 144–45.

CHAPTER TWO: THE EXISTENTIAL DIMENSION

1. Martin Esslin, *The Theatre of the Absurd* (New York: Doubleday, 1961), 18–19.

CHAPTER THREE: THE CONGLOMERATIVE EFFECT

1. "He owned, collected, and carefully studied Freud," William York Tindall told me, October 14, 1965. Tindall's work on Beckett includes "Beckett's Bums," *Critique: Studies in Modern Fiction* 12 (Spring-Summer, 1958): 3–15, and *Samuel Beckett* (New York: Columbia University Press, 1964).
2. See chapter 1 for a discussion of these works.
3. Nino Frank, "Il Mondo," in *Introductory Bulletin,* trans. Ciccio (November 1955): 5. Frank speaks of Beckett's sense of "happiness, perfection, [and] the absolute," in that state of "prelife immobility."
4. See, for example, Otto Rank, *The Trauma of Birth* (New York: Dover, 1993).
5. For Watt's lengthy dot and circle description of the painting in Erskine's room, see *Watt,* in *The Collected Works of Samuel Beckett* (New York: Grove, 1970), 128–29. It begins, "A circle, obviously described by a compass, and broken at its lowest point, occupied the middle foreground, of this picture. Was it receding? Watt had that impression. In the eastern background appeared a point, or dot. The circumference was black. The point was blue, but blue! The rest was white. How the effect of perspective was obtained Watt did not know. But it was obtained. By what means the illusion of movement in space, and it almost seemed in time, was given, Watt could not say. But it was given. Watt wondered how long it would be before the point and circle entered together upon the same plane. . . . And was it not rather the circle that was in the background, and the point that was in the foreground? . . . Who knows, they might even collide, . . . a circle and its centre in search of each other, or a circle and its centre in search of a centre and a circle

respectively, or a circle and its centre in search of . . ." See Henri Bergson, *Mind-Energy,* trans. H. Wildon Carr (New York: Henry Holt, 1948), and id., *The Creative Mind: An Introduction to Metaphysics,* trans. Mabelle L. Andison (New York: Philosophical Library, 1946).

6. Freud, *The Interpretation of Dreams,* trans. James Strachey (New York: Avon Books, 1998), 530, 526–46. Freud further says of secondary revision, "[It] behaves in the manner which the poet maliciously ascribes to philosophers: it fills up the gaps in the dream-structure with shreds and patches. As a result of its efforts, the dream loses its appearance of absurdity and disconnectedness" (528).
7. Although Freud comments on unconscious thoughts and dreams throughout *The Complete Psychological Works of Sigmund Freud,* trans. James Strachey (London: Hogarth Press, 1984), see vols. 4 and 5 for the "Interpretation of Dreams." Except where I cite material from the *Complete Works,* I have tried to limit my citations to the paper edition of *The Interpretation of Dreams* (New York: Avon, 1998). Particularly pertinent to this discussion are chap. 1, part E, "The Distinguishing Psychological Characteristics of Dreams"; chap. 6, "The Dream Work," which discusses condensation, displacement, secondary revision, and other dream techniques; and chap. 7, part E, "The Primary and Secondary Processes."
8. The present discussion may affect the debate, heightened since Beckett's death, regarding why directors must, or perhaps may not, adhere to Beckett's elaborate production notations.
9. See Freud, *Interpretation of Dreams,* 626–48; Ernest Jones, *The Life and Work of Sigmund Freud* (New York: Basic Books, 1957), 323–28; *Comprehensive Textbook of Psychiatry,* ed. Harold I. Kaplan and Benjammin J. Sadock (Baltimore: Williams and Wilkins, 1995), 2 vols.; *Language and Thought in Schizophrenia,* ed. J. S. Kasanin (New York: Norton, 1964); *American Handbook of Psychiatry,* ed. S. Arieti (New York: Basic Books, 1974); and H. F. Searles, *Collected Papers on Schizophrenia and Related Subjects* (Madision, Conn.: International Universities Press, 1988). See also Bert O. States, *The Rhetoric of Dreams,* trans. Alan Sheridan (London: Tavistock Publishers, 1987); and David Foulkes, *The Grammar of Dreams* (New York: Basic Books, 1978).
10. It has long been accepted that schizophrenics use primary process, or the language of dreams or the unconscious, in their everyday speech. See note 9 for corroborating sources.

11. Freud, *Interpretation of Dreams,* 530, 313.
12. Freud, *The Complete Psychological Works,* 73. In a sense, Beckett presents what Freud would call the "manifest content" of the dream, the dream as reported by the dreamer. Psychic energy or the "dream work" has been translated into visual play, the manifest content. We, like the patient interacting with an analyst, through our associations with the material presented before us, look for the underlying meaning, the "latent content" of the dream/play. Understanding, for example, that a dream results from a conflicted wish, we can easily understand that "Let's go," followed by "*They do not move*" is the result of a compromise between impulse and inhibition.
13. Quoted in Dougald McMillan and Martha Fehsenfeld, *Beckett in the Theatre* (New York: Riverrun Press, 1988), 115.
14. This frequently quoted passage, which clearly relates to *Godot,* is as follows: "I am interested in the shape of ideas, even if I do not believe them. There is a wonderful sentence in Augustine. I wish I could remember the Latin. It is even finer in Latin than in English. 'Do not despair; one of the thieves was saved. Do not presume; one of the thieves was damned.' That sentence has a wonderful shape. It is the shape that matters." See Harold Hobson, "Samuel Beckett—Dramatist of the Year," *International Theatre Annual* 1 (1956): 153–55.
15. Quoted in McMillan and Fehsenfeld, *Beckett in the Theatre,* 141.
16. Jack MacGowran once said, "I think sometimes the roles are reversed. I think Estragon is the one who has read and known everything and thrown it away. . . . Vladimir, who appears to be the brighter of the two, is, in fact, the half-schooled one madly trying to find out answers, pestering Estragon the whole time. . . . Estragon has read everything and dismissed it." Quoted in Jonathan Kalb, *Beckett in Performance* (Cambridge: Cambridge University Press, 1989, 26).
17. Democritus's concept of nothing and the significance of sleeping and dreaming, as I propose throughout, suggest several paradoxes in his statement.
18. Freud discusses such "unifications" of persons ("identifications") and of things ("composition"). He says that a series of identifications may lead to a "composite figure," which I shall discuss shortly. See *The Interpretation of Dreams,* 354–61.
19. In the Schiller-Theater production, which Beckett directed, the question of his beard as red is added. See chapter 7 below.

CHAPTER FOUR: THE CONGLOMERATIVE VOICE

1. Except where indicated, all biblical citations are taken from the King James version.
2. Traditionally, the biblical text would say that a woman "conceived again and bore. . . ." Instead, it reads that Eve "bore Cain . . . And she again bore his brother Abel" (Genesis 4:1–2). See *The Interpreter's Bible* (New York: Abingdon Press, 1952), 1:517.
3. That this tale has lent itself to varying and opposing interpretations is indicated by the vast amount of material published on the subject. Even a partial listing of secondary sources would be outside the scope of this book. The New Testament comments upon this tale in Hebrews 11:4. Cain's offering would seem to be rejected because he lacks a pure heart: "By faith Abel offered unto God a more excellent sacrifice than Cain, by which he obtained witness that he was righteous, God testifying of his gifts." Numerous Christian commentators believe that the chapter is directed to "examples of faith [which] mean primarily holding fast to hope." See *The Oxford Study Bible: Revised English Bible with the Apocrypha,* ed. Jack Suggs, Katharine D. Sakenfeld, and James R. Mueller (New York: Oxford University Press, 1992), 1529. That this tale of excessive punishment and persecution remained troublesome at least as far back as 1 B.C. is apparent in "The Wisdom of Solomon," in which Solomon attributes both Cain's and Adam's fall to their lack of wisdom of "the Spirit of the Lord," rather than to their lack of righteousness. See *Oxford Study Bible,* 10:1–4.

   Of particular interest to my discussion are the many Midrash commentaries (the vast compendium of ancient Jewish lore and homilies) on the inexplicability of God's rejection of Cain's gift. This, many assert, gives rise to Cain's blind violence against a judgment he cannot comprehend. Jonathan Ben Uzziel restates the quarrel between the brothers: "Abel said: 'My sacrifice was accepted because my good deeds exceeded yours.' Cain answered: 'There is no justice and there is no judge, there is no world-to-come and no reward or punishment for the righteous and wicked.' About this the brothers quarreled. Cain set upon his brother. Abel killed him with a stone." *Genesis Revisited* 22:8, as cited in Robert Graves and Raphael Patai, *Hebrew Myths: The Book of Genesis* (New York: McGraw-Hill, 1966), 91. Some scholars, cited in *The Torah: A Modern Commentary,* ed. Gunther Plaut (New York: Union of American Hebrew Congregations), 48n.2, explain Shimon's reluctant interpretation: "It is difficult to say such a thing (i.e., to read the text as it ought to be read) and the mouth cannot say it (as it would imply the blaming of God). Shimon compared the God-Cain-Abel triangle to two gladiators fighting before a king. The ruler could stop the contest any minute, but lets it proceed to the bitter, deadly end. Is he not, by his silence, involved in the killing?" His point would seem to be that having granted man moral freedom, God, in a sense, shares in man's transgression. Perhaps this is why he is silent. See also Yehezkel Kaufmann, *The Religion of Israel* (Chicago: University of Chicago Press, 1960), 295.

Harold Bloom views Cain as a rebel, not as a villain, and writes in *The Book of J* (New York: Grove Weidenfeld, 1990,) 66, defending Cain, "Now Yahweh said to Cain: 'Where is your brother, Abel?' 'I didn't know it is I,' he answered, 'that am my brother's workman.' "

On the other hand, the Koran speaks of Cain's repentance, Sura V:36 (The Table), like many religious scholars. Ruth Mellinkoff, in *The Mark of Cain* (Berkeley: University of California Press, 1981), reviews interpretation from the time of the Targen texts, Aramaic versions of the Hebrew Bible, that date back to 70 A.D. through the present. Honor Matthews, in *The Primal Curse* (New York: Schocken Books, 1967), focuses initially on Abel, "a type of Christ" (13), and turns to Cain when considering later systems of justice; Cain then became a "ceremonial" tragic figure. As early as the Miracle plays, audiences suffered with the speaker in his "lamentation," for example, in the Chester play:

> (84)
> Out! Out! alas! alas!
> I am damned without grace,
> Therefore I will from place to place
> . . . .
> (85)
> Foule hep is me befall:
> wheither I be in howse or hell,
> Cursed Cayne men will me call
> From sorrow may non me save.

Varying discussions regarding the actual mark on Cain, such as a tattoo or horn, are equally interesting. Opposing the view of Cain's mark as divine condemnation to perpetual wandering, isolation, and loneliness

—i.e., a scar that would align him with a vengeful and brutal tribe—are those arguments that the prophets bore such marks for protection (Zech. 13:4–6). Cain's act and his subsequent mark may reflect an act of communal sacrifice to revive the land, and as such, God would protect him. Marks are also discussed as indications of God's protection until one repents. See Gerhard von Rad, *Genesis: A Commentary* (Philadelphia: Westminster Press, 1961), 114, and Umberto Cassuto, *From Adam to Noah* (Jerusalem: Magnes Press, 1961), 304, and especially Mellinkoff, *The Mark of Cain*. Sir James Frazer, in *Folk-Lore in the Old Testament* (New York: Tudor Publishing, 1923), 44–45, has a particularly interesting comment regarding Cain's mark, for he believes that it protected Cain against Abel's ghost, "a mode of disguising a homicide, or of rendering him so repulsive or formidable in appearance that his victim's ghost would . . . not know him." Frazer continues: "This explanation has the advantage of relieving the Biblical narrative from a manifest absurdity [because] there was nobody to assail [Cain], since the earth was as yet inhabited only by the murderer himself and his parents. Hence by assuming that there . . . was a ghost instead of a living man, we avoid the irreverence of imputing to the deity a grave lapse of memory, little in keeping with the divine omniscience." That this tale of fratricide occurred in pagan mythology would seem to be common knowledge. In Egyptian legend, Seth slew Osirus; in a Canaanite tale, Mōte killed Baal; Romulus killed Remus; Edom, Amos; the moongod, a serpent (who, he later learned, was his brother). But in each, little detail follows. See Frazer, *Folk-Lore in the Old Testament,* which traces the myth through Europe, Asia, Africa, and Polynesia.

4. Elie Wiesel, *Messengers of God,* trans. Marion Wiesel (New York: Random House, 1976), 72–73.
5. Wiesel takes this from his study of the Midrash, *Messengers of God,* 54.
6. The number 7, for example, punctuates the chapter; Abel's name appears seven times, as do the words *brother* and *name*. Lameth, who kills Cain, is in the seventh generation from Adam, and the sevenfold vengeance is evoked; Cain lives to be 777. The number also has vast associations with lunar phenomena, evoked throughout the Bible. The word *fall* (and its inverse *uplift*), prevalent in *Godot* also as a verb and noun, is repeated: "And his countenance fell. . . . Why is thy countenance fallen?" If Cain does right, his face will be uplifted.
7. *The Bible: A Modern Commentary,* 44.

8. According to Numbers 3:46–47, the first child belongs to God and must be acquired from him.
9. See R. R. Wilson, *Genealogy and History in the Biblical World* (New Haven: Yale University Press, 1977); S. Gervitz, *Patterns in the Early Poetry of Israel* (Chicago: University of Chicago Press, 1963); Matthew Black, ed. *Peak's Commentary on the Bible* (London: Rowley, 1982); Julius A. Bewer, *The Literature of the Old Testament,* (New York: Columbia University Press, 1922); *The JPS Torah Commentary: Genesis,* trans. Nahum M. Sarna (New York: JPS, 1989).
10. *Peake's Commentary on the Bible,* among others, describes these "cities of refuge," as collection of tribes that gave each fugitive-member a brand, so he would be immediately recognized and protected. Some suggest that Cain was already an outlaw when he confronted Abel; others, that he began the Kenite tribe, the group of herdsman-smithies-wanderers, who lived to avenge their brothers. See n. 2 above.
11. To some, Cain is rebuked because his offering was made casually: it was not made with the same heartfelt love and respect to God shown by Abel. It would also appear that God often favors the younger child. One has only to think of Jacob and Essau, Joseph and his brothers, Ishmael, Aaron, and Reuben. Freud, in "Moses and Monotheism," *Complete Works,* 23:81, writes that "youngest sons occupied an exceptional position. . . . We seem to detect echoes in legends and fairy tales both of the expulsion of elder sons and of the favouring of youngest sons."
12. In calling sin "him," is he referring to the sin within Genesis 3, manifest in Satan? In fact, sin is connected with the Akkadian word for demon. See Ephraim A. Speiser, *Genesis* (Garden City: Doubleday, 1964), and the New English Bible.
13. Elie Wiesel, in *A Beggar in Jerusalem* (New York: Random House, 1970), 111, has a unique interpretation. He believes Cain kills Abel to stop all future warfare: He would have Abel say, " 'Let us fight so as to fight no more. Let us kill so as to conquer death.' Who knows, perhaps Cain himself aspired to be not just the first murderer in history but the last as well." Skinner, *Genesis,* 106, believes that Cain's unhappiness lay solely within himself. Quoted in *The Interpretive Bible,* 518.
14. See Hebrews 11:4 and n. 3.
15. See reference to Shimon in n. 3.
16. *The Bible: A Modern Commentary,* 48n.2. The editor writes, "The text

does not quote what was said. The Septuagint and Targum supply these words: " 'Come, let us go out into the field.' "

CHAPTER FIVE: THE LANGUAGE OF DREAMS

Note to epigraphs. Unless otherwise noted, all references to Freud's *Interpretation of Dreams* are cited from the Avon edition (New York, 1998); for these two epigraphs, see 564, 629. Continuing his discussion of the "absurd" in dreams, Freud wrote, 480, that dreams "are most often most profound when they seem most crazy. In every epoch of history those who have had something to say but could not say it without peril have eagerly assumed a fool's cap. The audience at whom their forbidden speech was aimed tolerated it more easily if they could at the same time laugh and flatter themselves with the reflection that the unwelcome words were clearly nonsensical."

1. Salomon Resnik, *The Theatre of the Dream,* trans. Alan Sheridan (London: Tavistock Publishers, 1987), 17–19. Resnik relates Freud's dream theory to a number of contemporary philosophers often connected with Beckett and, of particular interest, with psychoanalysts associated with the Tavistock, including W. R. D. Fairbairn, Melanie Klein, D. W. Winnicott, as well as Bion. Throughout *The Interpretation of Dreams,* Freud speaks of dreams as "dramatizations" of ideas, often using the word *absurd* to define the "mood of the dream thoughts, which combines derision or laughter with contradiction." See 470, 86–87, 65–67, 97. See also David Foulkes, *Grammar of Dreams* (New York: Basic Books, 1978), and Bert O. States, *The Rhetoric of Dreams* (Ithaca: Cornell University Press, 1988), and *Seeing in the Dark: Reflections on Dreams and Dreaming* (New Haven: Yale University Press, 1997). States has written a number of outstanding books on dreams as well as one about *Waiting for Godot* in which he does not discuss dreams: *The Shape of Paradox* (Berkeley: University of California Press, 1978). In *Seeing in the Dark,* he writes, "Dreaming and art-making . . . share a 'technique' of purification of waking experience. They are essentializing processes, as aestheticians say. [They ask] you to look at things you haven't been seeing" (6–7).
2. Although this information appears to be commonplace among psychiatrists and psychologists, the following will introduce the nonspecialist to generally accepted theories about unconscious functioning and the

rhetorical devices that characterize dreams, Freud's "royal road to the unconscious." In addition to *The Interpretation of Dreams,* see Freud's "Neurosis and Psychosis" and "The Loss of Reality in Neurosis and Psychosis," *General Psychological Theory,* trans. Joan Riviere (New York: Collier, 1963), 185–89, and 202–6, respectively. See also note 9, chap. 3. For quick reference to Freud's definitions of the components of the dream (which he frequently compares to a picture puzzle, or "rebus"), see, in *The Interpretation of Dreams,* his discussion of condensation (a "bizarre composite image or word"), 212, 261, 314, 318; of displacement (the shifting of one idea to another with no resemblance to the original, except in space or time, and with an often comic effect), 215, 340–44, 444; plastic representation (visual images of thoughts or concepts, "sometimes also in sensory modalities"), 432; reversals and turning of things and ideas into their opposite, 362; consonance and alliteration, 355.

Language and Thought in Schizophrenia, ed. J. S. Kasanin (New York: Norton, 1964), has an excellent collection of essays, including Norman Cameron, "Experimental Analysis of Schizophrenic Thinking" (on "asyndetic thinking"); Harry Stack Sullivan, "Language of Schizophrenia" (on the schizophrenic's compulsion to talk—for personal security, rather than for communication; on the autistic, narcissistic, individualized nature of unconscious language; on its "magic"); E. Von Domarus, "The Specific Laws of Logic in Schizophrenia" (on paralogic); and Kurt Goldstein, "Methodological Approach to the Study of Schizophrenic Thought Disorder" (on the use of concrete thinking and loss of boundaries between the self and world). On the inability to deal with generalizations in paralogical thought, see E. Hanfmann, "Analysis of the Thinking Disorder in a Case of Schizophrenia," *Archives of Neurology and Psychiatry* 41 (1939): 568–79.

See also *American Handbook of Psychiatry,* ed. S. Arieti (New York: Basic Books, 1974); Salomon Resnik, *The Theatre of the Dream,* trans. Alan Sheridan (London: Tavistock Publishers, 1987); Foulkes, *Grammar of Dreams;* Norman Cameron, "The Development of Paranoic Thinking," *Psychology Review* 50 (1943): 219–33; id., "The Paranoic Pseudo-Community," *American Journal of Sociology* 49 (1943): 32–39; J. S. Kasanin, "The Acute Schizoaffective Psychoses," *American Journal of Psychology* 3 (1937): 97; J. S. Kasanin and E. Hanfmann, "A Method for the Study of Concept Formation," *Journal of Psychology* 3 (1937): 521–40; Gordon Globus, *Dream Life, Wake Life: The Human Condition through Dreams* (Albany: State University of New York, 1987); Antonio R. Damasio, *Descartes' Error: Emotion, Reason and the Human Brain* (New York: Putnam, 1994); and J. Allan Hobson, *The Dreaming Brain* (New York: Basic Books, 1988). For an introduction to these concepts, with illustrations from literature, see Frederick J. Hoffman, *Freudianism and the Literary Mind* (Baton Rouge: Louisiana State University Press, 1945).

3. Colin Duckworth asked Beckett, "Is Lucky so named because he has found his Godot?" Beckett replied, "I suppose he is Lucky to have no more expectations," quoted in Dougald McMillan and Martha Fehsenfeld, *Beckett in the Theatre* (New York: Riverrun Press, 1988), 64.
4. Freud writes of conjunctions, with this his list, 347, in *The Interpretation of Dreams:* "Dreams have no means at their disposal for representing . . . logical relations. . . . The plastic arts of painting and sculpture labour, indeed, under a similar limitation as compared with poetry, which can make use of speech."
5. Beckett listed themes and diagrammed actors' movements in the *Regiebuch,* his production notebook for the 1975 Schiller-Theater production, which he directed. McMillan and Fehsenfeld, in *Beckett in the Theatre* (New York: Riverrun Press, 1988), have, in a sense, broken the code in deciphering Beckett's often arcane instructions. On the instances of waiting, see 91.
6. E. Von Doramus, "The Specific Laws of Logic in Schizophrenic," in *Language and Thought in Schizophrenia,* 110–11.
7. "I get warm when I run," followed by "quickness, blood, heart of deer, length, driven power, motorized cylinder, strength" is a frequently cited example. In waking, syndetic, or secondary process, all but one or two alternatives in a series would be eliminated; in asyndetic thought, the various alternatives are retained. A statement lacks logical linkage and even the imaginative connective of symbolic statement. See Norman Cameron, "Experimental Analysis of Schizophrenic Thinking," in *Language and Thought in Schizophrenia,* 52–54.
8. Typical of the breakdown of reality boundaries are somatic complaints, which concretely manifest an emotional state—a headache, for example, indicating that one's problems are literally splitting one apart.

Estragon's aching feet and Vladimir's pained loins function according to the same mechanism. See *Comprehensive Textbook of Psychiatry,* ed. Alfred M. Freedman et al. (Baltimore: Williams and Wilkins, 1975), 1:900.

CHAPTER SIX: "THE KEY WORD IS . . . 'PERHAPS'"

Note to epigraphs: The first, Beckett's description of his plays, was reported by Israel Shenker, "Moody Man of Letters." *New York Times,* May 6, 1956, sec. 2: 1–3. For Beckett's famous comment regarding the two thieves, see Harold Hobson, "Samuel Beckett—Dramatist of the Year." *International Theatre Annual* 1 (1956): 153–55.

1. See, for example, *Men of the Plain, Men of Destiny,* and *The Top of the Tide,* as well as *Two Travellers.*
2. See Samuel Beckett, "Hommage à Jack B. Yeats," *Les Lettres Nouvelles* (April 1954), and "An Imaginative Work," *Dublin Magazine* 11 (July-September 1936): 80–81. When Yeats was introduced to Beckett, he was called "the Cézanne of our times." For a fuller discussion of Yeats's influence on Beckett, see Lois Gordon, *The World of Samuel Beckett, 1906–1946* (New Haven: Yale University Press, 1996), chap. 4.
3. For a more lengthy discussion of this, see chapter 1.
4. For example, Michael Faraday's work inducing electric currents concluded that every unit of positive electrification is related to a unit of negative electrification, with the result that it is impossible to produce an *absolute* charge of electricity. James Clark Maxwell translated Faraday's ideas into mathematics and demonstrated how to reduce electrical and magnetic phenomena to stresses and motions of a material medium. At the end of the nineteenth century, a major debate concerned whether the universe was reducible to mathematical formulas or diagrams of phenomena. Faraday saw lines of force traversing space, while mathematicians saw centers of force attracting it. Along other lines, J. J. Thomson's theory of electrons challenged the Brownian randomness of matter; and although A. A. Michelson and E. W. Morley's experiment to find an influence between the earth's motion and the velocity of light failed, it anticipated Einstein in his work on relativity. Much of this, during a time when science was exalted, was common knowledge among the well educated.
5. In a letter to Alec Reid, shown to me on July 18, 1978. Of interest, Roger Blin recalled this from a conversation with Beckett: "He didn't know

what *God* meant. Maybe he meant *Godillots,* which means 'old shoes.' [Beckett] said, 'Estragon's old shoes, maybe that's what it is.' But I knew that adding *ot* in French, as in Godot, is often a way of showing a contempt, of ridiculing, at least." See "Interview with Roger Blin by Joan Stevens," in Lois Oppenheim, *Directing Beckett* (Ann Arbor: University of Michigan Press, 1994), 305.

6. Guy de Maupassant added that Monet was "no longer a painter but a hunter after the palpability of the universe." Monet also said, when his eyesight was failing, "I will paint almost blind, as Beethoven composed completely deaf." Interesting to this study, as well, his aspirations toward "oceanic sensation" have been related to Freud's *Civilization and its Discontents* and to a remark Freud made describing this feeling as a "true source of religious sentiment." See Romy Golan, "Oceanic Sensations," in *Monet in the Twentieth Century,* ed. Paul Hayes Tucker, with T. M. Shackelford and MaryAnne Stevens (New Haven: Yale University Press, 1998), 80. (Monet remarked, "My deepest intuitions toward spirit evoke absence and the void.")
7. Samuel Beckett, *Proust,* in *The Collected Works of Samuel Beckett* (New York: Grove, 1970), 48–49.
8. *An Augustine Synthesis,* arranged by Erich Przywara (New York, Harper, 1958), 77–78.

CHAPTER SEVEN: STAGING THE CONGLOMERATIVE EFFECT

1. Among Beckett's many productions, which he directed or assisted in directing, are *Godot*'s premiere at the Théâtre de Babylone in 1953, the 1961 London production at the Royal Court, and the famed 1975 Schiller-Theater production in Berlin, which he directed, assisted by Walter Asmus. The San Quentin Drama Workshop production in 1984 was based on his notebooks from the Berlin production; he joined Asmus during the last ten days of rehearsal. Dougald McMillan and Martha Fehsenfeld, *Beckett in the Theatre* (New York: Riverrun Press, 1988), clarify Beckett's complex *Regiebuch* from the 1975 Berlin production. Many of my references to it rely on McMillan and Fehsenfeld. Interpretive comments are my own. See also *The Theatrical Notebooks of Samuel Beckett,* ed. James Knowlson, vol. 1 (New York: Grove, 1994), which reproduces the *Regiebuch.*
2. In addition to his many notebooks are annotated texts from the San Quentin Drama Workshop production, Beckett's own, well-marked

copies of the Grove (1954) and Faber and Faber (1984) editions, as well as those of directors (such as Walter Asmus) and actors (Rick Cluchey, Bud Thorpe, Lawrence Held). See *The Theatrical Notebooks of Samuel Beckett,* ed. James Knowlson (New York: Grove, 1994), 1:467–68. Although not all of the changes in the Berlin and San Quentin Drama Workshop were consistent, Knowlson has taken hundreds of changes in both these productions and published a revised text of the play. As Knowlson acknowledges, since changes depended upon countless variables—e.g., different connotations after translation—it remains impossible to arrive at an absolutely final text. The following exemplify a few changes: in the original English text, Estragon usually responds to Vladimir's "We're waiting for Godot" with "Ah!" This has been changed to "Ah yes," "Good idea," "True," and "Fancy that." Also in the San Quentin Workshop production, "That's life" became "C'est la vie." In the Berlin and San Quentin productions, Godot's beard may be not just fair or black, but also red (connecting Godot to the brothel story in the play and therefore to the scatological). One of the most significant changes in Germany involved the beginning of the play. Vladimir, offstage in the English text, was placed upstage right, so there would be a parallel in the beginning of acts I and II. Estragon's mound was also changed to a stone. Beckett deleted Pozzo's smoking; gave him a lorgnette, instead of spectacles; and changed "Jupiter," Atlas's brother, to "Japetos," his father, thereby correcting Pozzo's reference in the text. Knowlson, *The Theatrical Notebooks,* xiii–xvii.

3. Ruby Cohn, in *Just Play: Beckett's Theater* (Princeton: Princeton University Press, 1980), 237, notes, "The spoken text must be not only letter-perfect, but punctuation-perfect; [Beckett would] stop an actor who elides a comma-pause." Roger Blin speaks for many of Beckett's directors: "Precision is next to Godliness in Godot." Rick Cluchey, who founded the San Quentin Drama Workshop, told me in a phone interview in 1991 that he had no choice but to "obey the Master," to scrupulously produce a play "just as Beckett wanted," where "the text is the text." Beckett's concern with production has prompted several excellent studies that survey productions in the United States and abroad and include directors' and actors' experiences with Beckett. In addition to Cohn, *Just Play,* see Jonathan Kalb, *Beckett in Performance* (Cambridge: Cambridge University Press, 1989); James Knowlson, *The Theatrical Notebooks*; and Lois Oppenheim, *Directing Beckett* (Ann Arbor: Univer-

sity of Michigan Press, 1994). One anecdotal report reveals a great deal about Beckett's attention to production details. He wrote to Roger Blin about Estragon's trousers (his "frock") at the end of *Godot:* "Just be kind enough to restore it as indicated in the text, and as we had agreed upon in rehearsal, and have the trousers fall completely around his ankles. This must seem stupid to you, but for me it is essential" (See Oppenheim, *Directing Beckett,* 297).

Walter Asmus, who has worked closest with Beckett, provides interesting material pertinent to this study, about how Beckett offered the characters "images for understanding their relationship." Although Gogo is to be associated with the tree, and Didi with the stone, as Beckett instructed, "That means they are connected, and at the same time there is always the tendency to go apart. [Beckett] used this image of the rubber band: they pull together by means of a rubber band and tear apart again, and so on—which makes sense if you have to make crossings onstage." Beckett added, " 'every word, one step,' and that tells the actor that there is not only an outer approach of moving this way, but also an inner approach of becoming more and more, say, tender or subtle in talking to one another. Things like that which tell something about the characters' relationship. . . . Gogo and Didi [know] exactly when they [are] hurting one another" (Kalb, *Beckett in Performance,* 175).

Also relevant to the overview of this book is Herbert Blau's response to the question of where *Godot* takes place. Blau cites a line from *Endgame:* "There's something dripping in my head" and goes on to say, "It's the dripping in the head from whence the drama comes, its deep structure" (Oppenheim, *Directing Beckett,* 56). Tom Bishop also speaks of the need for dialogue to appear as though it comes "out of the dark . . . colorless, . . . paused properly to achieve the purpose of 'emotional explosions' " (statement made at a symposium on Beckett and Joyce at New York University in 1991).

Many directors address Beckett's later work. To Xerxes Mehta, founder and artistic director of the Maryland Stage Company, the early plays retain "social and communal context," whereas the later ones are "sealed off from the world." I would suggest that many of Mehta's and the others' comments apply equally to *Godot,* if one defines connection with the world in terms of conscious and unconscious thought functioning. Mehta, for example, describes the late plays as "ghost-plays" or "hauntings." He continues, "What the spectator sees appears to come swimming out of blackness. [To me, Beckett's externalization of the unconscious life]." As such, I would borrow Mehta's language in stating that "the spectator experiences *the reality* of dream or unconscious experience" in the early as well as the late plays, although Beckett's dialogue and images are surely more nonreferential later. Most intriguing are Mehta's remarks on how he, as director, evokes a dreamlike environment in a work like *Play.* He simulates a spectral quality by creating a sense of absolute aural and visual sense deprivation in the audience. Before the play begins, darkness is "as absolute as it can be," recreating the darkness that is "part of the weave of the work." Similarly, Mehta's cancellation of sound and space in the theater leads the spectator "into a physical void." The spectator is assaulted and is "will-less to resist," feeling "on the edge of sanity." Mehta says that Beckett's "wraithlike images" on stage reinforce "the assault on reason." Time, place, and community are destroyed and turn the spectator inward. Performer and audience become one, in touch with the grief and terror of the human condition. Sound becomes babble, and the spectator subliminally feels the human story. The circular and consuming nature of each works's inner narrative is designed to frustrate the assertion of identity. Silences are most terrifying and they again destroy communion; in Mehta's words, silences are "yawning like a pit, creating extreme anxiety, and giving the word or sound that finally breaks a mythical force. Together, the visual and sonic tracks combine to create a single stark emblem of the human condition but subliminally undermine each other, disintegrating the whole into mystery and chaos" (*Directing Beckett,* 170–85).

Robert Scanlan, literary director of the American Repertory Theatre in Cambridge, Massachusetts, also concentrates on the late plays, asserting that Beckett writes in an essentially nonverbal medium. Actors must undergo the transitions from reading the script aloud (an "implied voice"), to listening to an inner voice (a "quoted voice"), and then to acting with the voice that is discovered through these stages—"the source of the voice"—a "looking glass, a mirror, of mystery and freedom"—"often a quest for the origin of voices." (Oppenheim, *Directing Beckett,* 149–52). One might substitute the unconscious for Scanlan's "source of the voice" in the early works. The Polish director and translator Antoni Libera believes that behind Beckett's every work is his belief in the Crucifixion but his rejection of the Resurrection and Redemption. As a result, Libera sets Beckett's plays "the night between the day of Crucifixion and the day of Resurrection, which represents a time without God." He continues, "[This] became the most important sign of his own life. He was born on Good Friday . . . died on Friday, this time two days before Christmas. . . . A life lived within such brackets is a sign in itself. It symbolizes failing to meet God." This could also be "the condition of contemporary man" (Oppenheim, *Directing Beckett,* 114). (Cohn, in *Just Play,* 34, mentions that Beckett annually celebrated the Crucifixion on April 13, his birthday.) In staging Beckett, Libera then combines this assumption with Giambattista Vico's "ingenious concept of language as the chief tool for man's self-transformation and the concept that the evolution of mankind proceeds along a spiral. At the same time he questions the overall message of this theory . . . [of] stages of development. . . . Beckett creates an image in which contemporary times are interpreted . . . as [going] on and on, [to] become more wearisome and gloomy" (Oppenheim, *Directing Beckett,* 114–15).

4. Pozzo and Vladimir speak about time in act II at stage center, and the hat-swopping and Vladimir's song occur there.
5. In the San Quentin Workshop Drama presentation, which Walter Asmus directed according to the *Regiebuch* from the Schiller-Theater Production. Beckett attended the last rehearsals and made final directorial decisions.
6. McMillan and Fehsenfeld, *Beckett in the Theatre,* 99. All subsequent references to the *Regiebuch* will be taken from this source.
7. Ibid., 55.
8. Walter Asmus, "Beckett Directs Godot," *Theatre Quarterly* 5 (Sept.-Nov. 1975): 19–26.
9. McMillan and Fehsenfeld, *Beckett in the Theatre,* 103.
10. Beckett's comment to Jean Reavey, August 1992, quoted in ibid., 16.
11. A video of the Schiller-Theater production is owned by the New York University Bobst Library; the San Quentin Drama Workshop production is available from the Smithsonian Institution.
12. Beckett added that the production should establish "at outset 2 cages dynamics, E. sluggish, V. restless and in perpetual separation and reunion with V/E." See ibid., 115.
13. See n. 4 above.

SELECTED BIBLIOGRAPHY

BIBLIOGRAPHY

Andonian, Cathleen Cullota. *Samuel Beckett: A Reference Guide*. Boston: G. K. Hall, 1989.

Brydan, Mary, Julian Garforth, and Peter Mills. *Beckett at Reading: Catalogue of the Beckett Manuscript Collection at the University of Reading*. Reading: Whiteknights Press and Beckett International Foundation, 1998.

Carpenter, Charles A. *Modern Drama Scholarship and Criticism, 1966–1980: An International Bibliography*. Toronto: University of Toronto Press, 1986.

Friedman, Melvin, ed. *Samuel Beckett Now: Critical Approaches to His Novels, Poetry, and Plays*. Chicago: University of Chicago Press, 1970.

Knowlson, James. *Samuel Beckett: An Exhibition*. London: Turret Books, 1971.

Lake, Carlton. *No Symbols Where None Intended: A Catalogue of Books, Manuscripts, and Other Material Relating to Samuel Beckett in the Collection of the Humanities Research Center*. Austin: The Center, 1984.

Murphy, P. J., Werber Huber, Rolf Breuer, Konrad Schoell. *Critique of Beckett Criticism: A Guide to Research in English, French, and German*. Columbia, S.C.: Camden House, 1994.

The Samuel Beckett Collection: A Catalogue. Reading: University of Reading, 1978.

BIOGRAPHY

Bair, Deirdre. *Samuel Beckett: A Biography.* New York: Harcourt, Brace, Jovanovich, 1978.

Brater, Enoch. *why beckett.* London: Thames and Hudson, 1989.

Cronin, Anthony. *Samuel Beckett: The Last Modernist.* London: HarperCollins, 1996.

Gordon, Lois. *The World of Samuel Beckett.* New Haven: Yale University Press, 1996.

Gussow, Mel. *Conversations With and About Beckett.* New York: Grove, 1996.

Harmon, Maurice, ed. *No Author Better Served: The Correspondence of Samuel Beckett and Alan Schneider.* Cambridge: Harvard University Press, 1998.

Juliet, Charles. *Conversations with Samuel Beckett and Bram van Velde.* Leiden, Netherlands: Academic Press, 1996.

Knowlson, James. *Damned to Fame.* New York: Simon and Schuster, 1996.

O'Brien, Eoin. *The Beckett Country.* Dublin: Black Cat Press, 1986.

ON PERFORMANCE

Homan, Sidney. *The Audience as Actor and Character.* Lewisburg: Bucknell University Press, 1989.

Kalb, Jonathan. *Beckett in Performance.* Cambridge: Cambridge University Press, 1989.

Knowlson, James, ed. *The Theatrical Notebooks of Samuel Beckett.* Volume 1. *Waiting for Godot.* New York: Grove, 1994.

McMillan, Dougald, and Martha Fehsenfeld. *Beckett in the Theatre.* New York: Riverrun Press, 1998.

Oppenheim, Lois, ed. *Directing Beckett.* Ann Arbor: University of Michigan Press, 1994.

CRITICISM

Books marked with a bullet deal primarily with Beckett's later works or his fiction or both, but may be of interest to the reader studying *Godot.*

•Abbott, Porter A. *Beckett Writing Beckett: The Author in the Autograph.* Cornell: Cornell University Press, 1996.

Acheson, James. *Samuel Beckett's Artistic Theory and Practice.* New York: St. Martin's Press, 1997.

Alvarez, A. *Samuel Beckett*. New York: Viking, 1973.

Andonian, Cathleen Cullota. *The Critical Response to Samuel Beckett*. Westport, Conn.: Greenwood Publishing, 1998.

Barnard, C. G. *Samuel Beckett: A New Approach*. New York: Dodd Mead, 1970.

•Begam, Richard. *Samuel Beckett and the End of Modernity*. Stanford: Stanford University Press, 1996.

Ben-Zvi, Linda. *Samuel Beckett*. Boston: Twayne, 1986.

•Brater, Enoch. *Beyond Minimalism: Beckett's Late Style in the Theater*. New York: Oxford University Press, 1987.

•——. *The Drama in the Text: Beckett's Late Fiction*. New York: Oxford University Press, 1994.

Bryden, Mary. *Samuel Beckett and the Idea of God*. New York: St. Martin's Press, 1998.

Burkman, Katharine H. *The Arrival of Godot: Ritual Patterns in Modern Drama*. Rutherford, N.J.: Fairleigh Dickinson Press, 1986.

Busi, Frederick. *The Transformations of Godot*. Lexington: University of Kentucky, 1980.

Butler, Lance St. John. *Samuel Beckett and the Meaning of Being: A Study in Ontological Parable*. London: Macmillan, 1984.

Coe, Richard N. *Samuel Beckett*. New York: Grove, 1964.

Cohn, Ruby. *Back to Beckett*. Princeton: Princeton University Press, 1973.

——. *A Beckett Canon*. Ann Arbor: University of Michigan Press, 2001.

——. *The Comic Gamut*. New Brunswick: Rutgers University Press, 1962.

——. *Just Play*. Princeton: Princeton University Press, 1980.

•Connor, Steven. *Samuel Beckett: Repetition, Theory and Text*. New York: B. Blackwell, 1988.

Cormier, Ramona, and Janis L. Pallister. *Waiting for Death: The Philosophical Significance of Beckett's "En Attendant Godot."* University, Alabama: University of Alabama Press, 1979.

Cousineau, Thomas. *Waiting for Godot: Form in Movement*. Boston: Twayne, 1989.

Duckworth, Colin. *Angels of Darkness*. London: Allen and Unwin, 1972.

Ellmann, Richard. *Nayman of Noland*. Washington, D.C.: Library of Congress, 1986.

Essif, Les. *Empty Figure on an Empty Stage: The Theatre of Samuel Beckett and His Generation*. Bloomington: Indiana University Press, 2001.

Esslin, Martin. *The Theatre of the Absurd*. New York: Doubleday, 1961.

Federman, Rayond, and John Fletcher. *Samuel Beckett: His Works and His Critics*. Berkeley: University of California Press, 1968.

Fletcher, John. *Samuel Beckett's Art*. London: Chatto and Windus, 1967.

——. *Waiting for Godot, Endgame, Krapp's Last Tape*. London: Faber, 2000.

Fletcher, John, and John Spurling. *Beckett: A Study of His Plays*. New York: Hill and Wang, 1972.

•Gontarski, S. E. *The Intent of "Undoing" in Samuel Beckett's Dramatic Texts*. Bloomington: Indiana University Press, 1985.

Graver, Lawrence. *Samuel Beckett: "Waiting for Godot."* New York: Cambridge University Press, 1989.

Harvey, Lawrence. *Samuel Beckett: Poet and Critic*. Princeton: Princeton University Press. 1970.

Henning, Sylvie Debevec. *Samuel Beckett's Critical Complexity*. Lexington: University Press of Kentucky, 1988.

Hesla, David H. *The Shape of Chaos*. Minneapolis: University of Minnesota Press, 1971.

Hoffmann, Frederick J. *Samuel Beckett: The Language of Self*. Carbondale: Southern Illinois University Press, 1962

Jacobsen, Josephine, and William R. Mueller, *The Testament of Samuel Beckett*. New York: Hill and Wang, 1964.

•Jones, David Houston. *The Body Abject: Self and Text in Jean Genet and Samuel Beckett*. New York: Peter Lang, 2000.

Kennedy, Andrew. *Samuel Beckett*. New York: Cambridge University Press, 1989.

Kenner, Hugh. *A Reader's Guide to Samuel Beckett*. London: Thames and Hudson, 1973.

——. *Samuel Beckett: A Critical Study*. New York: Grove, 1961.

——. *Flaubert, Joyce, and Beckett: The Stoic Comedians*. Boston: Beacon Press, 1962.

Kern, Edith. *Existential Thought and Fictional Technique: Kierkegaard, Sartre, and Beckett*. New Haven: Yale University Press, 1970.

•Knowlson, James, and John Pilling. *Frescoes of the Skull: The Later Prose and Drama of Samuel Beckett*. London: John Calder, 1979.

Knowlson, James. *Light and Darkness in the Theatre of Samuel Beckett*. London: Turret, 1972.

Levy, Shimon. *Samuel Beckett's Self-Referential Drama: The Three I's*. Basingstoke: Macmillan, 1990.

•Locatelli, Carla. *Unwording the World*. Philadelphia: University of Pennsylvania Press, 1990.

Lyons, Charles R. *Samuel Beckett*. London: Macmillan, 1983.

Mercier, Vivian. *Beckett/Beckett*. New York: Oxford University Press, 1977.

•Moorjani, Angela. *Abysmal Games*. Chapel Hill: North Carolina Studies in the Romance Languages and Literatures, 1982.

Morrison, Kristin. *Canters and Chronicles: The Use of Narrative in the Plays of Samuel Beckett and Harold Pinter*. Chicago: University of Chicago Press, 1983.

•Murphy, P. J. *Reconstructing Beckett: Language for Being in Samuel Beckett's Fiction*. Toronto: University of Toronto Press, 1990.

•Oppenheim, Lois. *The Painted Word: Samuel Beckett's Dialogue with Art*. Ann Arbor: University of Michigan Press, 2000.

Pilling, John. *Beckett before Godot*. New York: Cambridge University Press, 1997.

——. *Samuel Beckett*. London: Routledge and Kegan Paul, 1976.

Poutney, Rosemary. *Theatre of Shadows: Samuel Beckett's Drama 1956–1976*. Gerrards Cross, England: Colin Smythe, 1988.

Reid, Alec. *All I Can Manage, More Than I Could: An Approach to the Plays of Samuel Beckett*. Dublin: Dolmen Press, 1968.

Robinson, Michael. *The Long Sonata of the Dead: A Study of Samuel Beckett*. London: Hart-Davis, 1969.

Scott, Nathan A. *Samuel Beckett*. New York: Hillary House, 1965.

States, Bert O. *The Shape of Paradox*. Berkeley: Univerity of California Press, 1978.

Trezise, Thomas. *Into the Breach: Samuel Beckett and the Ends of Literature*. Princeton: Princeton University Press, 1990.

•Uhlmann, Anthony. *Beckett and Poststructuralism*. New York: Cambridge University Press, 1999.

Webb, Eugene. *The Plays of Samuel Beckett*. Seattle: University of Washington Press, 1972.

•Weisberg, David. *Chronicles of Disorder: Samuel Beckett and the Cultural Politics of the Modern Novel*. Albany: State University of New York Press, 2000.

Worth, Katharine. *"Waiting for Godot" and "Happy Days": Text and Performance*. Basingstoke: Macmillan, 1990.

——. *Samuel Beckett's Theatre: Life Journeys*. Oxford: Clarendon, 1999.

Zurbrugg, Nicholas. *Beckett and Proust*. Buckinghamshire: Colin Smythe, 1987.

COLLECTIONS OF ESSAYS

Beja, Morris, S. E. Gontarski, and Pierre Astier, eds. *Humanistic Perspectives*. Columbus: Ohio State University Press, 1983.

Ben-Zvi, Linda, ed. *Women in Beckett: Performance and Critical Perspective*. Urbana: University of Illinois Press, 1990.

Birkett, Jennifer, and Kate Ince, eds. *Samuel Beckett*. New York: Longman, 2000.

Blau, Herbert. *Sails of the Herring Fleet: Essays on Beckett*. Ann Arbor: University of Michigan Press: 2000.

Brater, Enoch, ed. *Beckett at Eighty/Beckett in Context*. New York: Oxford University Press, 1986.

Bryden, Mary, ed. *Samuel Beckett and Music*. New York: Clarendon Press, 1998.

Buning, Marius, and Lois Oppenheim, eds. *Beckett in the 1990s: Selected Papers from the Second International Beckett Symposium, held in The Hague, 8–12 April, 1992*. Atlanta: Rodolphi, 1993.

Buning, Marius, et al. *Beckett Versus Beckett*. Atlanta: Rodolphi, 1998. (In *Samuel Beckett Today/Aujourd'hui* series).

——. *Samuel Beckett: Crossroads and Borderlines*. Atlanta: Rodolphi, 1994. (In *Samuel Beckett Today/Aujourd'hui* series).

Burkman, Katherine, ed. *Myth and Ritual in the Plays of Samuel Beckett*. Rutherford, N.J.: Fairleigh Dickinson Press, 1987.

Butler, Lance St. John, ed. *Critical Essays on Samuel Beckett*. Brookfield, Vt: Ashgate Publishing, 1993.

——. *Rethinking Beckett: A Collection of Critical Essays*. London: Macmillan, 1990.

Calder, John, ed. *Beckett at Sixty: A Festschrift*. London: Calder and Boyars, 1967.

——. *As No Other Dare Fail: For Samuel Beckett on his 80th Birthday*. New York: Riverrun Press, 1986.

Cohn, Ruby, ed. *Casebook on "Waiting for Godot."* New York: Grove, 1967.

——. *"Waiting for Godot": A Casebook*. London: Macmillan, 1987.

Connor, Steven, ed. *"Waiting for Godot" and "Endgame."* New York: St. Martin's Press, 1992.

Esslin, Martin, ed. *A Collection of Critical Essays*. Englewood Cliffs: Prentice-Hall, 1965.

Friedman, Melvin J. *Samuel Beckett Now*. Chicago: University of Chicago Press, 1970.

Gontarski, S. E., ed. *On Beckett: Essays and Criticism*. New York: Grove, 1986.

——. *The Beckett Studies Reader*. Gainesville: Univerity Press of Florida, 1993.

Graver, Lawrence, and Raymond Federman, eds. *Samuel Beckett: The Critical Heritage*. London: Kegan Paul, 1979.

McCarthy, Patrick A. *Critical Essays on Samuel Beckett*. Boston: G. K. Hall, 1986.

Morot, Edouard, Howard Harper, and Dougald McMillan, eds. *Symposium on Samuel Beckett: The Art of Rhetoric, from the Meeting at the University of North Carolina*. Chapel Hill: U.N.C. Department of Romance Languages, 1976.

Oppenheim, Lois. *Samuel Beckett and the Arts: Music, Visual Arts, and Non-print Media*. New York: Garland, 1999.

Oppenheim. Lois, and Marius Buning, eds. *Beckett On and On: Papers Presented to the Second International Beckett Conference, Held in the Hague, April 22, 1992*. Rutherford, N.J.: Fairleigh Dickinson University Press, 1996.

Pilling, John, ed. *The Cambridge Companion to Beckett*. Cambridge: Cambridge University Press, 1994.

Pilling, John, and Mary Bryden, eds. *The Ideal Core of the Onion*. Bristol: Longdunn Press, 1992.

Schlueter, June, and Enoch Brater, eds. *Approaches to Teaching "Waiting for Godot."* New York: Modern Language Association, 1991.

Smith, Joseph H., ed. *The World of Samuel Beckett*. Baltimore: Johns Hopkins University Press, 1991.

Sussman, Henry, and Christopher Devenney. *Engagement and Indifference: Beckett and the Political*. Albany: State University of New York Press, 2001.

Wilmer, S. E., ed. *Beckett in Dublin*. Dublin: Lilliput Press, 1992.

Worth, Katharine, ed. *Beckett the Shape Changer*. London: Routledge and Kegan Paul, 1975.

SAMUEL BECKETT PUBLICATIONS, SPECIAL ISSUES OF JOURNALS DEVOTED TO BECKETT

American Book Review 12.6 (January-March 1991).
The Beckett Circle
Chicago Review, a section of 33.2 (1982).
Critique 519–20 (August-September 1990).
Hermathena 141 (1986).
Irish University Review 4.1 (1984).
James Joyce Quarterly 8 (1971).
Journal of Beckett Studies
Journal of Modern Literature 6.1 (1977).
Modern Drama 9.3 (1966); a section of 19.3 (1976), 25.3 (1982), 28.2 (1985).
Perspective 11.3 (1959).
Romance Studies 11 (Winter 1987).
Samuel Beckett Today/Aujourd'hui
Theater Heute 2 (February 1990).

VIDEOS: *WAITING FOR GODOT*

Beckett Directs Beckett. A Performance of the San Quentin Drama Workshop. Washington, D.C.: Smithsonian Institution Press Video: 1990–92. (*Waiting for Godot, Krapp's Last Tape, Endgame*).

En attendant Godot. Directed by Walter Asmus. Paris: Editions du Seuil, 1990.

Waiting for Godot. Original production directed by Alan Schneider. New York: Grove, 1961; New York: Applause, 1997.

Warten auf Godot. Schiller-Theater production. Mainz, Germany: ADF, 1976.

VIDEOS: BIOGRAPHY AND RELATED MATERIAL

Asmus, Walter. *Conversations on Beckett: Teachers' Guide*. New York: Visual Press and Cameras Continentales, 1988.

Beckett Directs Beckett. Discussion by Walter Asmus, Herbert Blau, Kathleen Woodward, Robert Corrigan, Martin Esslin, John Fuegi, Rich Cluchey, and others. University of Maryland. New York: Visual Press and Cameras Continentales, 1992.

Jack MacGowran and Edward Albee Talk of Samuel Beckett. New York: New York Public Library Theater on Film and Tape Archive, 1971.

O'Mordha, Sean. *As the Story was Told*. London: BBC, 1996; Princeton: Films for the Humanities Press, 1992.

Reilly, John. *Waiting for Beckett*. New York: Global Village, 1993.

John Reilly Associates. *The Beckett Project*. Global Village, 1992–99. Includes biography, *Quad I* and *II, Not I,* and *What's Where,* film clips of other works, Beckett's letters, and archival photos and footage.

Thirtynine Today. Max Wall discusses with James Knowlson his 1975 experiences acting in *Krapp's Last Tape,* directed by Patrick Magee. London: British Universities Film and Video Council, 1978, 2000.

MUSICAL SETTINGS OF BECKETT'S WORK

Crowder, Henry. *Henry-Music: Poems by Nancy Cunard, Richard Aldington, Walter Lowenfels, Samuel Beckett [and] Harold Acton*. Paris: Hours Press, 1930.

Fein, Ron. *Music for Non-Cooperative Ensembles*. Based on *Waiting for Godot*. Hollywood, Fla.: Euphonic, 1987.

Feldman, Morton. *For Samuel Beckett*. London: Universal Edition, 1987; Kairos, 1999.

——. *Neither: An Opera in One Act on a Text by Samuel Beckett*. London: Universal Edition, 1977; CD, Bad Wiesse: Col Legno, 2000.

Glass, Philip. String Quartet no. 2. Based on *Company*. New York: Nonesuch, 1995.

Haubenstock-Ramati, Roman. *Credentials, or 'Think Lucky.'* London: Universal Edition, 1963.

Hollinger, Heinz. *Come and Go*. Portland: Accord, 1994.

——. *Words and Music. Morton Feldman,* vol. 2. Washington, D.C., NPR, 1990.

Horvitz, Wayne B., and Mark E. Miller, *"Cascando": Words and Music*. New York: Theatre for Your Mother, 1979.

Katzer, Georg. *Godot is Coming, but is Going Again*. Scores for instrumental ensembles, for piano. Bad Schwalbach, Germany: Edition Gravis, 2000.

Kessner, Daniel. *"Texts for Nothing:" A Musical-Literary Theatrical Stream after Samuel Beckett*. New York: New York Public Library, 1982.

Kim, Earl. *Earthlight*. New York: New World Records, 1977.

Mantler, Michael. *Many Have No Speech*. Song cycle. Words by Samuel Beckett. New York: Watt, 1988.

Reynolds, Roger. *Selections*. Disk 1. "An opera of the mind" based on Beckett's early work. Acton, Mass., Newma, 1996.

Wilkinson, Marc. *Voices, from the Play "Waiting for Godot."* London: Universal Edition, 1960.

INDEX